Warring Parents, Wounded Children, and the Wretched World of Child Custody

Cautionary Tales

Joseph Helmreich and
Paul Marcus

PRAEGER

Westport, Connecticut
London

Library of Congress Cataloging-in-Publication Data

Helmreich, Joseph, 1983–
Warring parents, wounded children, and the wretched world of child custody : cautionary
tales / Joseph Helmreich and Paul Marcus.
    p. cm.
    Includes bibliographical references and index.
    ISBN: 978–0–313–34973–7 (alk. paper)
    1. Children of divorced parents—United States.   2. Divorced parents—United
States.   3. Custody of children—United States.   I. Marcus, Paul, 1953–   II. Title.
    HQ777.5.H45   2008
    306.88—dc22   2007035424

British Library Cataloguing in Publication Data is available.

Library of Congress Catalog Card Number: 2007035424
ISBN: 978–0–313–34973–7

First published in 2008

Praeger Publishers, 88 Post Road West, Westport, CT 06881
An imprint of Greenwood Publishing Group, Inc.
www.praeger.com

Printed in the United States of America

The paper used in this book complies with the
Permanent Paper Standard issued by the National
Information Standards Organization (Z39.48–1984).

10 9 8 7 6 5 4 3 2 1

Copyright Acknowledgment

The authors and the publisher gratefully acknowledge permission to reprint four lines from
the song "Ballad in Plain D," by Bob Dylan. Copyright © 1964; renewed 1992 Special Rider
Music. All rights reserved. International copyright secured. Reprinted by permission.

To my family, whose love, support and enormous talent guided and inspired me through the completion of this book.
JH

To the pained children of these stories. May they find some peace of mind as adults.
PM

Contents

Introduction

According to David Emery, a modern chronicler of folklore and urban legends, a *cautionary tale* is a "fable with a moral message warning of the consequences of certain actions or character flaws."[1] So, "The Boy Who Cried Wolf" is a *cautionary tale* about the dangers of recklessness and deceit. Likewise, the tale of "King Midas and the Golden Touch" is a *cautionary tale* that warns us about the dangers of greed. Cautionary tales often have tragic dimensions and the primary message is almost always the same: Don't behave the way these people did or this might happen to you.

Over the past several decades, much ink has been spilled over the modern-day horror of child custody disputes. Most of what's been written has been fairly accurate and helpful. However, what these numerous books and articles have failed to give us is a truly in-depth, real-life understanding of the *tragedy* of these conflicts and the selfish personal motivations and behavior that end up causing so much of the devastation. Instead, they are essentially "how-to" books that give useful advice about legal strategies, but say precious little about the deep underlying forces that drive most of the original problems. Hollywood has done a far better job at conveying some of the tragedy and human errors involved, but movies, even good ones like *Kramer vs. Kramer* and *The Squid and the Whale*, can only show us a narrow, distorted, and overly stylized version of what really goes on. Also, they tend to focus solely on white, upper-class citizens, leaving the rest of the country sitting alone in their darkened theaters.

---

[1] http://Urbanlegends.about.com/library/glossary/bldef-cautionary.htm

This book is an attempt to shed some light on the realities of the modern-day custody battle through the use of cautionary tales. There is a dynamic power to storytelling. Stories are accessible, memorable, and there is an almost mystical way in which stories can often reveal the truth and illuminate a path forward much more effectively than simple guides, prescriptions, or "advice" ever could. It seems that to truly understand the nature and gravity of certain mistakes, we sometimes have to watch them as they are made and see the tragedy unfold.

The following stories are all rooted in actual cases, though names and details have been changed. They have been culled from many years of experience as a professional, court-appointed child custody evaluator for Family and Supreme courts. To better understand what that means, here is a brief word on the nature of custody evaluation:

A forensic psychologist or evaluator is someone who applies "scientific and clinical expertise . . . to legal issues in legal contexts embracing civil, criminal, correctional, or legislative matters." Such legal issues related to mental disorders include evaluating and providing testimony in "malpractice litigation, will contests, personal injury litigation, competency determinations (both civil and criminal), criminal responsibility, and presentencing hearings."[2] A *child custody evaluator* is a very specific kind of forensic psychologist who is assigned by the court to psychologically evaluate the family. When the investigation is complete, the evaluator submits a written report to the judge with recommendations based on what he or she thinks to be in the best interests of the children. Sometimes the judge decides to, more or less, go along with the evaluator's suggestions. Other times, as we will see in some of these cases, he or she chooses to ignore them completely.

The cases covered in this book follow people of every kind of ethnic and economic background as they engage in struggles with their former spouses over issues like custody, visitation, relocation, allegations of child and spousal abuse, physical threats, etc. Some of these tales are overwhelmingly distressing, others offer glimmers of hope, but all can be learned from. Together, they give the reader an inside view of the self-destructive human flaws—the selfishness, blindness, and downright stupidity—that play such large roles in people's downfalls. In addition, through commentaries at the end of each chapter, the book offers in-depth analyses and concrete practical instructions on what to do and what *not* do in similar situations.

---

[2]*The American Psychiatric Press Textbook of Psychiatry.* Second edition, edited by Robert E. Hales, Stuart C. Yudofsky, and John A. Talbott. Washington, DC: American Psychiatric Press, 2005, p. 1327.

Nietzsche once said, "The function of tragedy is not to provide catharsis, as Aristotle saw it, but to offer an exemplary spectacle of glorious waste." Indeed, glorious waste is the best way to describe the dominant theme in most stories of custody dispute. The truth is that even though the system is admittedly fallible, some would even say corrupt, citing examples of uncaring judges, greedy lawyers, incompetent law guardians, and pompous custody evaluators, most custody-visitation disputes are still fairly simple and could be easily resolved by reasonable people. Yet, this too often fails to occur. When strong emotions like anger, jealousy, and unrequited love come into play, people who seem well intentioned can become so irrational and selfish that they lose total sight of what is in the best interests of themselves and their children. Love gets lost. Hurt and vengeful, the wounded parties wind up wreaking total havoc on the lives of those around them.

Most of the following stories are tragic. But if they can caution us about the future and perhaps even teach us something about ourselves, then, from out of our failures, something redemptive can emerge. If through examining the mistakes of the past, we can arrive at some kind of greater understanding, then through what was lost, something important may be gained.

"And so it did happen like it could have been foreseen,
The timeless explosion of fantasy's dream.
At the peak of the night, the king and the queen
Tumbled all down into pieces."

—Bob Dylan, "Ballad in Plain D"

CHAPTER 1

The Gordons

"There is no glory in battle worth the blood it costs."
—Dwight Eisenhower

"I'll be honest with you, Paul," said Mike, as we both sat down to the table. "It's not a good situation." Mike Lillienfeld was a friend from college and the two of us were meeting for lunch to catch up on old times and, more importantly, to discuss my latest assignment, the Gordon case. I had only been put on it days before and needed to catch up quick. Mike, on the other hand, had spent the last ten years as the law clerk for the judge handling the case and could give me a unique insider's perspective.

"It's a lifer," Mike said, his eyes scanning the lower portion of the menu. "These parents—they're not a shitty divorce case. They are *the* shitty divorce case, *par excellence.*"

He looked up and smiled, but I couldn't bring myself to smile back. I leaned back in my seat and sighed. It was going to be a long few weeks. When I had met with Judge Williams, days before, she had told me, "Dr. Marcus, I want you to do anything—and I mean *anything*—to keep these lunatics out of my courtroom." Now, Mike's words in the coffee shop had confirmed what had been my fear back then: I had just been handed the case from Hell.

The Gordons were an interesting and highly intelligent couple. Robert Gordon, shy, unassuming, and handsome, met Jane Schiff back in 1986, when Jane had been representing a man named Thomas Black in a malpractice suit against Holy Cross Hospital of Long Island City. At one point during the trial,

Robert, defending Holy Cross, had objected to Jane's cross-examination tac-
tics, declaring, "Your honor, the counsel is clearly attempting to hyperbolate
the facts." Upon hearing this, Jane turned to Robert, stared him in the eyes,
and said, "I am *sure* that is not a word"—and he fell for her right then and
there. While Robert was quiet and reserved, Jane was bubbly and assertive
and the combination made for what appeared to be the perfect odd couple.
The two wasted little time in getting married and, soon after, Jane gave birth
to a beautiful baby boy, whom they called Noah. About three years later, she
gave birth again, this time to twin girls, Mindy and Sarah.

One morning, about six months after having given birth, Jane was preparing breakfast for the children, when Robert walked in, somewhat solemnly,
and sat down at the table.

"Hey there," Jane said, smiling at the suit he was wearing, which she'd
bought for him the week before. Robert didn't respond at first, almost as
though he hadn't heard her. Then, he returned the greeting with a charac-
teristically soft-spoken, "Hello." Then, eyes lowered to the tabletop, he told
her he wanted out.

Why did Robert Gordon, less than four years into his marriage to an attractive, intelligent, and sophisticated young woman, suddenly want a divorce?
Unfortunately, it is here, at this question, that our solid, cohesive narrative
suddenly diverges into two separate tales. This is not surprising. In almost all
divorces, the reasons behind the initial split are a matter of bitter contention.
But in this case, the discrepancies in the two accounts are particularly wide. In
the interest of fairness, we will now take a look at both sides of the situation,
separately.

According to Robert, his marriage to Jane, at the point at which he left it,
was essentially already dead. There was simply no more passion from his side
of things, no more excitement and, most importantly, no more love. Instead,
what Robert felt was a severe sense of suffocation. When they'd first met and
Jane had corrected his English in the middle of a crowded courtroom, he had
found it charming. But now, he realized, he should have right away seen her
for what she was: controlling. Jane was bossy and rigid and, in truth, didn't
even have very much in common with him. Yes, the marriage was no less
his mistake than hers. But should he have to pay for this mistake for the
rest of his life? Did it even make any sense to stay married to a person one
didn't love?

His timing for leaving was a tad inappropriate, he could understand that,
could concede that point. Yes, maybe he shouldn't have run off just when
she'd recently given birth to twins—there was certainly something to be said
for sticking around at least another year or so. But, the truth was, he genuinely

felt that the longer he stayed, the harder it would be on everyone else when he *did* leave. Actually, the twins had represented a last-ditch effort to save the marriage. Robert had thought that having another child together might spark some new life into the dying relationship, might resuscitate his withering feelings for Jane. But after Mindy and Sarah were born and his feelings did not change, he decided it was better to end it all as soon as possible, before any more damage could be done. This is what he did and, for the most part, he did not regret the decision.

According to Jane, however, Robert left her for a completely different reason. According to Jane, Robert left for one reason and one reason only: so he could openly sleep with her best friend, Laurie. Oh yes, sure, Robert could claim that he only developed feelings for Laurie *after* he'd left, but come on. He walks out on Jane right after she gives birth and then shacks up with Laurie only a month and a half later? It was all too symmetrical, too perfectly timed. Before it crashed and burned, Robert and Jane's marriage had seemed, to Jane, perfectly normal and perfectly happy. At the very least, Jane was content and while Robert could sometimes be a bit cold and had a sense of humor not entirely unlike that of a dead fish, he still generally acted lovingly toward her and the children. And so Jane never would have suspected that he could be cheating on her—let alone with Laurie Alexander, her best friend from Fordham Law.

Amusingly, the new couple would later tell people that Laurie and Jane had been mere acquaintances at school, but surely they knew this was patent bullshit. Was it not Jane who Laurie had come running to the night her brother Gary took an unexpected leap off the Brooklyn Bridge? And was it not Jane who Laurie had called every other night for about a month after she'd moved from Manhattan to Williamsburg and was finding herself miserable there?

But why should Jane really care? If that was the real Robert, a liar and a cheat, then who needed him anyway? And if he wanted to be with Laurie, and Laurie, after everything Jane had done for her, wanted to be with him, then the two low lowlifes deserved one another. Jane couldn't waste any time worrying about it and she didn't. About a year and a half later, she met Jerry Lang, a stockbroker from Staten Island and, after several months of dating, the two were married. Jerry, a caring and responsible man, became stepfather to Noah and the twins, and life for the former Jane Gordon began anew.

In general, the children sided more with Jane than with their father. When I talked with Mindy and Sarah, both fifteen, they told me that they tended to believe their mother's version of how the marriage broke down—that Robert had had an adulterous affair with Laurie—but that they preferred not to think about this very much.

"We try to pretend that we come from a *normal* family," Mindy said. "It's kind of like a game we play. Or a joke."

They told me that their father had always been pretty heavily involved in their lives, but that they often resented him, especially when he would get into loud, embarrassing arguments with their mother in public. Over the years, the girls had witnessed many disturbing fights between their parents. These usually took place in the driveway of their home, when Robert was picking them up or dropping them off. Oddly enough, even though he was typically a quiet man, Robert was almost always the instigator in these clashes. In fact, one time, during an argument outside the twins' school, he yelled so loudly that the police were called to intervene.

Mindy and Sarah conveyed a tremendous amount of respect for the way their mother had managed to raise them by herself for so many years (i.e., before Jane met her new husband). But, it should be noted, they did not hate their father. He was a decent dad and they appreciated the time he spent with them. Still, in addition to the resentment they felt over his bad behavior, they often found him to be demanding. They didn't like the way he was always pressuring them to be with him, when they would sometimes rather be spending time with friends. And they resented both parents for often pulling them into arguments by asking them to convey messages to each other.

In general, I got the impression that what they really resented, more than anything else, was their overall situation. What Mindy and Sarah wanted was a regular, conventional family life—and they didn't feel like they were living one.

If the twins had complicated, conflicting feelings about their father, Noah's outlook was simple: he wanted nothing to do with the man. Noah, now eighteen and still living with his mother, had effectively broken off contact with his father about six years before, and he had no interest in revisiting the relationship now, nor did he have any interest in the current courtroom fighting ("Would everyone just let me get on with my life?" he moaned, over the telephone). It was only after much prodding and pleading that I was able to get him to come down to my office.

As he shifted anxiously in a large green easy chair, Noah explained that his father's recent legal maneuverings, which included an attempt to gain more access to the children, represented nothing more than a new way of torturing Jane. "Don't forget, this is the same asshole who walked out on my mother when she had three small kids to raise," he noted.

Noah struck me as a perceptive and intelligent young man. He was actually about to start his first semester at Cornell (in an accelerated mathematics program) and I could imagine him doing fine there. But there was one matter on which I disagreed with him. While Robert may not have been a saint, I did believe that his desire to strengthen his relationship with the kids was genuine. For example, even if according to the twins he had a tendency to be overbearing, Robert had made significant efforts to remain an active figure in his daughters' lives.

As for his relationship to Noah, I had actually witnessed Robert's eyes well up with tears as he recalled the pain of repeatedly trying to reconnect with Noah over the years and being rejected. They had once enjoyed a fairly positive relationship ("Back when he was a kid, before she brainwashed him into thinking I was the Devil"), and it was unclear exactly how the relationship had gone south, though it seemed that as Noah had gotten older, he had grown more attached to his stepfather and began to look at the way Robert had treated his mother with increasing disdain. I got the impression that in some ways, Noah had felt no less abandoned by his father's walking out than Jane had and that his own rage was almost a direct mirror image of Jane's.

I asked Noah if Jane had spoken often about his father when Noah was growing up.

"She talked about him and no, she didn't hide her feelings about him, but make no mistake about it: She did *not* brainwash me," he said, picking up on my most immediate suspicions. "I'm an adult now and I come to my own conclusions. And trust me, Dr. Marcus. The man is no good."

Such was Noah's immovable position on the matter. Several days after meeting with him, I read in the court documents that Noah had been brought to a psychiatrist, five years before, when his father had been pursuing custody. The psychiatrist had recommended that Noah not be forced to even *visit* with his father and that doing so could prove extremely dangerous, psychologically speaking.

Now, however, forcing Noah to confront his father was no longer even a possibility, because he was legally an adult. However, it was clear to me that it was very much in Noah's best interest to reestablish his connection to his father. Not doing so could have profound long-term effects on his self-esteem and self-concept, his relationship to authority figures in general, and perhaps even his relationship to his own future children.

It would clearly be a difficult task, but I hoped that if I played my cards right, pulled out all my old tricks and perhaps even experimented with some new ones, I might be able to help bring about some kind of reconciliation for this family. Noah was tough and very angry. But I'd met others like him before and many had eventually warmed up and come to accept their parents as human beings, warts and all. Maybe, I hoped, the same thing would happen here.

The situation now was extremely delicate. At the time I was called in, both parents had long been remarried, but it was all too clear that neither had really moved on with their lives. Their latest courtroom battles had recently gotten so far out of control that the judge, with the parents' consent, had asked me to intervene and conduct a series of meetings with both parents, together, *outside* of the courtroom, to see if we could resolve some of these problems without a trial. The judge had correctly understood that the root of the problem lay not only in particular issues of money or custody, but in unfinished *personal business*. And that was why a psychologist was so necessary.

At this particular point, each parent had a specific demand of the other. Robert and Laurie had recently been given teaching posts at a New York law school and Jane was requesting that they help pay for Noah and the twins' education using Laurie's new college tuition benefits (they were already using Robert's). Robert and Laurie adamantly refused, claiming Jane had treated them horribly over the years and that she was now trying to use these tuition benefits as a bargaining chip.

Robert, for his part, was demanding expanded and unimpeded visitation with Mindy and Sarah and access to Noah (with an eye toward reconciliation) and was threatening to sue for custody if he did not obtain these things. I felt like I had just been hired as a referee for a Las Vegas boxing match and I was wondering how I could step into the middle of this thing without getting hit myself.

Robert Gordon and Jane Silver had not been in the same room together—at least not without lawyers, clerks, or judges—in over a decade. Now, as the two of them sat there, on opposite sides of my office, I was struck by how calm they each seemed. Sure, there was tension in the room, but it was not nearly at the level I'd imagined it would be. It seemed that my advice prior to the sessions—that they use this time to focus on the issues at hand and not try and dredge up ghosts of the past—was actually being heeded. I proceeded with the session.

We began with a relatively simple issue. According to Robert, Jane had recently been interfering with his visitations with the twins (the only children willing to see him). I had investigated this matter on my own, speaking to both Jane and the children, and had concluded that Jane *was* indeed interfering with the visitations, though not on a technical or legal level and not intentionally. Now, as I sat there and listened to Jane going on about the absurdity of Robert's claims, the tension in the room did begin to rise a little bit.

"I have never once—never *once*—denied him his right to visit with his daughters." Jane said, deliberately avoiding eye contact with her ex-husband.

Robert jumped in: "What about just last month, when you scheduled a visit to your sister's beach house right on one of my days?"

Jane turned to him and answered, "I told the girls it was up to *you* if they could go. You told me you wanted them and I let you have them and I went to my sister's myself!"

Robert rolled his eyes and Jane leaned back in her chair, smiling, satisfied by his silence. But then, when I turned to her and asked, "But isn't forcing Robert to become the bad guy a form of interference?" She didn't respond and I felt confident that she understood what I meant and that this kind of thing would probably not happen again.

The surprisingly good progress and better-than-expected behavior on the part of the parents continued and, several weeks into the sessions, I finally felt ready to bring up the more contentious subject of Noah's tuition. In this issue, it was Robert who was on the defensive. According to Jane, Robert had agreed in their divorce settlement to make diligent efforts to try and obtain scholarships or other stipends for the children's education, in addition to his regular payments of child support. Thus, if Robert had access to more tuition benefits (which he now did, through his wife, Laurie) then, according to Jane, he had a genuine legal obligation to use them for Noah's education. Jane contended that the fact that Robert and Laurie were not utilizing these benefits was needlessly costing her hundreds of thousands of dollars and even more in psychological distress. Furthermore, she claimed that Robert and Laurie's behavior in this matter had increased the bitterness between Robert and Jane to the point that it was beginning to have a very negative impact on the children, who seemed increasingly depressed.

Robert, using technical terms that I could only barely understand, strongly disputed the notion that he was legally required to utilize the benefits. He also pointed out that it was a bit hard to believe that Jane was so desperate for money when her husband was driving around in a brand new Lexus (a fact, which hadn't escape my attention either). And while he acknowledged that the current fighting was probably unhealthy for the children, he pointed out that this did not mean that *he* should be the one to give in. I was reminded, in that instant, that I was not simply dealing with two extremely angry parents, but also, two extremely gifted lawyers.

Robert leaned back in his chair and stared out the window.

"I don't want my children to suffer, Doctor," he said. "But you've got to understand, the way this woman has treated me and my wife over the past ten years makes it virtually *impossible* for us to give in to these demands."

I nodded, barely suppressing a smile. Robert had just said *exactly* what I had wanted to hear. He had admitted, clearly and plainly that he was putting his own anger and resentment ahead of the best interests of his children. And this made my job so much easier. I remained silent for a few moments, pretending to be absorbing what Robert had said, but really only planning my next move.

"Robert," I said, finally breaking my silence, "I understand that Jane may have caused a lot of pain for both you and your wife and I'm sure that's been terrible. But do you really think it's fair that because you suffered, the children should now have to suffer as well?"

He was silent and so I continued: "You tell me you're heartbroken over Noah's rejection of you. But don't you think if you suddenly took the high road and agreed to pay this money—even if you don't really have to and even if her husband is driving a fancy car—that it might be a step in a positive direction? And that it might make your son *think* a little bit, on his *own*, about what kind of father you really are?"

Robert quietly contemplated what I had just said and it seemed to me that this had never occurred to him before and was coming across to him as something of a revelation. Taking advantage of the situation and attempting to infuse it with a little more momentum, I turned to Jane and asked her if she could possibly imagine—in the event that Robert gave in to her current demands—helping to repair the relationship between father and son. Because no matter what Noah had said about being an adult now who could come to his own conclusions, it was still quite obvious to everyone that Jane exerted a strong influence over her son. After several moments of thought, Jane answered that yes, she could imagine herself helping to bridge the gap between Robert and Noah. Satisfied with all the recent turns of events, I called the session to a close.

Later that night, at approximately one in the morning, Noah Gordon received a telephone call on his personal phone line, which took him out of a very pleasant dream. Disoriented and annoyed, Noah reached for the receiver and put it to his ear.

"Hello?" he said.

There was silence. Then, the voice on the other end spoke:

"Noah, it's Dad."

Noah rubbed his eyes.

"What do you want?" he asked, and Robert, nervous and stuttery, responded:

"I just—I would like to meet up and chat. Like we used to. Maybe we can catch a Met game or something, I don't care where we do it."

Noah clenched his jaw and squeezed his pillow like a stress ball.

"What makes you think I want to meet up?" he asked.

"Noah, I'm going to give your mother the benefits. Laurie's benefits. I'm going to put in all the money for Cornell."

His father's voice was shaky, but starting to sound a bit more confident. Noah sat up in bed and leaned against the wall. For a moment, he said nothing. Then, slowly and steadily, he began to speak:

"Listen to me now, because I'm going to say this once and once only. I don't want your money. I just want you completely out of my life. Please don't try to help me or bribe me because I'll always see you for what you are. A total asshole."

And with that, Noah hung up the phone and went back to sleep.

Days later, I met with Laurie Gordon. Robert had left a message on my machine conveying a sudden change of heart and a determination not to give Jane "even a lousy cent" and I was feeling desperate. I was hoping against hope that perhaps Robert loved Laurie even more than he hated Jane, and that if I could convince Laurie to reconsider about the money, she could convince Robert to reconsider as well.

Laurie arrived early and as we began to talk, it quickly became clear to me that Laurie's views on Jane, reportedly her former best friend, were even harsher than her husband's:

"The woman is a leech, a parasite," Laurie explained. "Even back when she was married to Robert, it was always 'buy me this,' 'get me this.' Now, she's up to it again, demanding all this money when everyone knows she's loaded."

Laurie was particularly embittered toward Jane for having smeared her and Robert's names in the legal circles they all traveled in, and for bad-mouthing her to Noah and the twins. She told me that she would never, *ever*, allow her own tuition benefits to wind up in Jane's pocket.

Shortly before the end of the session, Laurie shared with me what she thought this was really all about:

"It's not about money," she said. "It's about *him*."

According to Laurie, Jane, deep down, still loved Robert and wanted him back—even though they were both long remarried. Laurie said that while Jane may have seemingly gone on with her life, she had never truly let go. For Jane, somewhere in the deepest, most repressed recesses of her mind, Robert still represented the perfect husband—the one man who could actualize all of her dreams for love and happiness.

But while Laurie's observations were insightful and accurate, I was distracted by something else, something fascinating that I had only just begun to notice. Maybe her eyes were a different color, and she was certainly taller, but Laurie, when one stopped to look, bore an incredibly striking resemblance to

Jane! Even beyond her physical appearance, her speaking style was exactly the same and it was incredible to me that Robert could have left one woman for the other, when the two seemed so similar.

Thus, as Laurie was trying to explain what Robert meant to Jane, I was busy pondering what *Laurie* meant to *Robert*. It seemed that, in Laurie, Robert had found a less overbearing variation on Jane. But that didn't really fit, because Laurie didn't come across as especially passive or submissive, or even noticeably less forceful than Jane. So what was the difference? I didn't know and the whole situation struck me as bizarre. I couldn't make sense of it and decided I wasn't going to try.

During my final session with Robert and Jane, Robert was particularly quiet and somber. Then, in the middle, as Jane and I were discussing the technicalities of her work schedule, Robert suddenly put his head into his hands and began to weep. Jane and I stopped talking and turned to him. Robert looked up, with as pained an expression as I have ever encountered in all my years of doing therapy.

"How?" he asked Jane, his voice soft and broken. "How could you do this to me? How could you be so cruel as to turn my own son against me like this?"

Jane was silent and expressionless.

"Why did you have to do it?" he went on, pleading. "Why this horrible revenge? I just don't understand. You have a new life, a new husband that you love, so *why*?"

Jane stared at him for several seconds, cold and hard, then looked down at the floor. "Jerry's a good man," she said, almost under her breath. "But I don't love him."

"Because you love me." Robert said.

Jane looked up at him, almost startled by his words, and then suddenly, she began to laugh. And then, just as suddenly, the laughter stopped.

"Are you out of your mind?" she asked, her eyes suddenly incredibly wide. "I *hate* you. You promised me that you'd be with me forever, that you'd take care of me. Then one day you walk into the room and you tell me that you're leaving me, abandoning me to raise three small children all by myself! You discarded me like an old, beat-up car, so you could go screw my best friend while everybody looked on and laughed. No, I don't love you, Bob—I don't love anyone! I can't love anyone, not after what you did to me. Not my husband, not even my children. I can't love anyone because I can't *trust* anyone. And now you sit there crying like a four-year old and you want me to feel sorry for you that your son doesn't want to kiss and make up? You can go fuck yourself. You *ruined* me."

Robert stared at her for several moments, positively stunned, and then slowly put his face back into his hands and continued to sob. I leaned back in my seat. Jane was shaking now, trying not to break down. I wanted to take control, to be the doctor, to say something. But there wasn't anything to say.

Three days later, I received a FedEx delivery from Robert's attorney, Chris Seeger, indicating that he and Robert both felt that it was not in keeping with my court-ordered mandate to be dealing with the financial issues between Robert and Jane—only custody and visitation—and that Robert would be withdrawing from the sessions. Around the same time, Seeger delivered the court a new set of legal papers. In these documents, Robert accused Jane of visitation interference, demanded custody of the twins, and declared that Laurie's tuition benefits would under no circumstances be utilized to pay for the education of Jane and Robert's children. The case would continue and Mindy and Sarah's dreams for a "normal life" would have to wait. Robert and Jane had gone right back to where they seemed to be most comfortable: at war with each other.

REFLECTIONS

The case of Jane, Robert, and Noah was a high-order triple tragedy. Jane was irreversibly wounded by Robert, "ruined" as she said, by his sudden, massive, and decisive abandonment and betrayal. Jane's basic trust and self-esteem were so damaged that she could no longer truly allow herself to feel love for another person ever again. Instead, her primary emotions alternated mostly between fury and despair. Robert, as a result of his ill-conceived, ill-timed, and utterly selfish behavior toward Jane and the children, lost his son. Robert's inner life, like Jane's, was characterized by riveting pain and rage. Noah's tragedy was that he lost his father, a man who, while deeply flawed, had tried in good faith and with some measure of regret for his prior actions, to reach out to him. By his own decision and in his own way, Noah punished his father for his "sin," his deceitful abandonment and betrayal of the family. Noah's hurt from being thrown over by his father evoked a palpable rage that was unlikely to ever go away and he would probably never have any contact with Robert for the rest of their lives.

The case of the Gordons demonstrates a major point about what not to do if you are planning on leaving your marriage and getting a divorce. It is very common in a disintegrating marriage that one of the parties begins an affair, perhaps to get back at their spouse or for some other impulsive reason. Don't do it! Or at the very least, don't get *caught* doing it. And never, *ever*, let your spouse or children know that this affair was consecutive with the separation. Only after you have been separated for about a year and the fighting has ended and the wounds have been sufficiently licked should they be made aware of the new relationship. I say this because if your spouse finds out, or construes the timeline and your actions in such a way that it *looks like* you left them for another, all hell can break loose. A man or woman scorned is someone who will pay you back big time, as Jane did to Robert by influencing their son against him. Also, as was the case with Noah, the children are often likely to feel personally betrayed, in addition to the anger they feel over what one parent did to the other.

This fatal dynamic, having a man or woman "in the wings" as a bridge to get out of a lousy marriage, was brought home to me again, just recently. In one of my cases, there was a couple whose marriage had been terrible for over twenty years. In fact, the wife had told me (in front of her husband!) that when he touched her, it felt like a rattlesnake stroking her. She indicated in one session that she no longer wanted to have their routine, obligatory once-a-week intercourse, and that her husband should go find himself a "some young slut to fuck," instead. The husband and wife could thus live together as roommates, creating the appearance of a normal marriage, until their daughter went off to college.

The husband took his wife's advice and found himself a girlfriend and fell in love with her and decided to marry her. But when his wife found out about this, that her husband had actually listened to her and now wanted out of the marriage, she was outraged. She quickly turned their daughter against him as well, telling her the whole story in a mean-spirited and wholly distorted fashion. Thus, both mother and daughter ultimately rewrote history, transforming a very troubled man into a "lowlife bastard" who had dumped his wife and daughter for a "whore." The broken-hearted father has not spoken to his daughter for more than eight years.

Another thing the Gordon case clearly demonstrates is how easily the legal system can become the medium for warring parents to play out their unfinished personal business at the expense of their children. Because of all of their unresolved hurt and pain, Robert and Jane continued their litigation for over a decade, making everything much worse for the children and themselves. This "dance of death" would probably never end. As my friend Mike had indicated in the coffee shop, the Gordons were truly "lifers."

CHAPTER 2

The O'Connells

"Betrayal is the only truth that sticks."

—Arthur Miller

As Mrs. O'Connell leaned in seductively, I found myself feeling suddenly uncomfortable. She was naturally beautiful, that much was obvious, but her close-fitting blouse and shirt, her transparent high heels, and the revealing way she crossed her legs were all starting to create a very distinct impression in me. Rose O'Connell, mother of Tim, Sean, Casey, and Liz O'Connell, ex-wife of Manhattan plumber, Brady O'Connell, was going to try and use her sexuality to win me to her side. I knew this was not going to work. But then, as I listened to her story, I began to realize that if even half of what she was saying were true, this woman, no matter what she looked like, was deserving of extreme sympathy. Like many of the stories I came across in this line of work, hers involved a fairly normal life that slowly began to darken and change shape until it resembled something else entirely.

Rose O'Connell was born in Ireland in 1954 to wealthy Catholic parents who immigrated to the United States about a decade and a half later. In America, Rose's life was pleasant. Her mother was kind and caring and her father, though extremely overprotective, cherished her as his little princess. At the time she met Brady, she was just out of high school and still a virgin, but Brady was taken by her innocence and the two dated for several months, during which he wined her, dined her, and spoiled her completely. Rose's parents were not particularly impressed with Brady' profession, plumbing, but they respected him as an enterprising immigrant. He was someone who had come to this country with next to nothing and could now afford a Mercedes, a beautiful apartment, and a wallet stuffed with hundred-dollar bills. Six months to the night of their first date, Rose and Brady got married in a small, intimate ceremony and moved into a spacious home in Maspeth, Queens, which Brady reconstructed and enlarged himself.

It was only months into their marriage when things began to get a little bit strange for Rose. Brady was loving and extremely generous, but, as time went on, he began to become oddly sexually demanding. He would come home in the middle of the day and then, after a cup of coffee, suddenly suggest that they "do it," right then. He would increasingly request that they have anal intercourse, something Rose *did not* enjoy, and would all but ignore her protests. He would insist on incorporating sexual appliances like dildos into their love life and practically force Rose to watch pornographic videos with him, after which the two would engage in "rough" sex, which he frequently liked to have in the early evenings, on demand.

Naturally dutiful and submissive, Rose felt like there was very little she could do. Brady's powers of persuasion were extremely strong and he frequently portrayed himself as a sort of *sexual sage* who would teach her the ways of the world and redeem her from her sexually repressive traditional Catholic upbringing. Soon, Rose and Brady had children of their own and Rose began to feel like she was leading a double life. She was a caring and responsible mother by day and then an obedient "love slave" by night. Yet, though she felt sexually oppressed by Brady, she still loved him as her husband, and loved their children as well, and was, if not entirely happy, not entirely unhappy either.

It was the summer of 1989 and Rose was preparing fresh corned beef for Brady when it occurred to her that his fiftieth birthday would be coming up shortly. She reminded him of this and, always eager to please, asked what he would like as a gift. Her husband was silent a few moments and then, suddenly relaxed, answered that he would like for them to return to Majorca, a Spanish island, where the two often vacationed together. In Majorca, he added, there was something very special he wanted her to do for him. She asked him what it was and Brady leaned back in his chair, smiled.

"I want you to have sex with another man. While I watch."

Actually, this was not an entirely shocking request. Many times in the past, Brady had asked her to describe fantasies about other men while she and him were engaged in intercourse. And at least twice, he had suggested the possibility of having a *ménage a trois* and had once asked Rose if she might consider having sex with a woman, while Brady looked on and "got off." In all of these cases, he had backed down in the face of Rose's objections. But now, he was asking her to sleep with another *man* and something about the look in his eyes told her that if she said no, he would be more than a little disappointed. No, he would not strike her, nor would he even yell at her. That wasn't how Brady worked. Instead, her refusal would create a strong air of negativity that would permeate their relationship in subtle ways. With every interaction, every dress she asked him to buy, there would be this feeling, hovering above, that she had really let him down. This was Brady's birthday wish. He wanted it very badly. It was weird, it was sick, but she couldn't bring herself to say no.

Majorca was sunny and beautiful, as usual, but Rose could pay little attention to aesthetics. Her mind was completely preoccupied with "the game." Brady had already suggested the man with whom she would be sleeping (a friend and associate of his) and now, she was to pretend to seduce him, as Brady coached her and looked on. Standing in a tight, yellow bikini, Rose finally spotted Carlos, making his way toward her from across the beach. She slowly raised and lowered her sunglasses, seductively, as per her instructions. Carlos walked over to her and extended his hand. "Your husband is one sick fuck," he said and the two walked off together to Carlos' motel room.

The whole thing lasted no more than twenty minutes. Brady was not there; Rose had been too embarrassed and Brady had finally conceded to stay back at the villa. Now, she was doing it, actually *doing it*, and feeling positively sick. When they were finished, her face was covered with tears and Carlos told her to stop crying because it was making him feel "weird." She felt disgusting, like a machine, like a robot with no will of its own and only one function.

When she returned to her villa, still whimpering, Brady was sitting outside, waiting for her. He paid no attention to her tears, asking for all the details, so they could finish the game. Then, as they walked inside, he told her to take off all her clothes. When she asked him why, he said, "Because I want to fuck you while your body is still warm from his." He then forced her to have sex with him, right then and there, pushing her up against the living room wall, a fitting end to an excruciating night.

Six months later, on another island, Rose was again made to seduce a stranger, this time a young man named Diego. Once again, she was to meet him on the beach. This time, though, the experience was very different. Diego was handsome, charming, thrilling, and, unlike Brady, lasted more than thirty seconds in bed. Sex with Diego was a pleasure and Rose looked forward to doing it again, which she did, several times, at Brady's urging. However, as Rose's feelings for Diego grew, describing the details to her husband became more and more uncomfortable. Even worse, every time she slept with Diego, Brady would insist on having sex with her immediately afterward and during the intercourse with Brady, she would inevitably find herself fantasizing about Diego. However, she did not want to tell Brady about any of this because she was afraid he would become enraged and, even more terrifying, might not let her continue to see Diego.

About three weeks later, Brady instructed Rose to bring Diego to America for a vacation, at Brady's expense. Perhaps he was thinking about a "ménage a trios," or maybe he thought he'd finally be able to convince Rose to let him watch them. But then, when he saw how comfortable Rose was with the arrangement and how eager Diego was to come to the States, he suddenly cancelled the plans. Was Diego in love with his wife? Was she in love with Diego? The possibility had never even occurred to Brady before and he now went into a complete panic. At first, he responded to the threat by being excessively nice to Rose, buying her things, romancing her. But that soon gave way to resentment and the couple's marriage began to irreversibly deteriorate. They would fight, often loudly and openly, and "divorce" became a recurring word in these quarrels. As is often the case, the tension between Rose and Brady quickly trickled down to the children and the O'Connell home became an increasingly uncomfortable place to be.

One afternoon, Rose came home from a tennis match to find her middle son, Sean, crying in the living room. She sat down beside him on the couch, put her arm around him, and he flinched and pulled away. Then he turned to her, a sudden softness in his eyes.

"Is it really true, Mom?" he asked. "Did you really cheat on Dad? Did you really have an *affair*?"

Rose didn't know what to say. She was absolutely shocked. "No!" she cried, practically choking on the words.

"But Dad told us!" Sean yelled. "He told us *everything*!"

Rose was outraged. Brady had apparently told all three sons, over lunch, that their mother had had an affair with a man named Diego and that that's why their family life was now going down the toilet. How could he do that?! And now, how could she do anything about it? Should she tell them the truth? She thought about that, but when she imagined herself doing it, walking into the kitchen and announcing to the children that their father had asked her to have sex with other men, that their father whom they loved so much was actually a sick pervert, she realized she just couldn't.

Over the next few weeks, Rose asked for a divorce, Brady moved out and the remaining O'Connell household deteriorated into a war zone. Tim, Sean, and Casey took their father's side completely and treated their mother with contempt, ignoring all chores and disobeying all of her rules. Liz was the only one who had no real knowledge of the "affair," but she still had a vague idea that her mother had done something *shameful*, and the relationship between mother and daughter began to strain as well.

Brady, meanwhile, took advantage of the boys' still living with Rose to use them as spies. At their father's urging, the boys would go through their mother's drawers, record her telephone conversations, and sometimes even read her mail, which mortified Rose and made her even more frustrated that she had to keep the real truth about her relationship with Diego—that it was all Brady's fault and had barely lasted a few weeks—to herself. By the time she came to see me, she was at her wits' end, robbed of her privacy, completely demonized and with no control whatsoever over her life.

I listened to this bizarre story with a combination of shock and empathy. I imagined Rose's inner turmoil—the injustice of being controlled and victimized and then being portrayed as the victimizer, as the sinful one, and turned into a pariah in her own home. Rose O'Connell's story was painful, a true tragedy and there was only one problem with it:

Brady O'Connell denied practically every word of it.

When I brought him into my office, several days later, he laughed as he listened to elements from his wife's version of the events, commenting, "She's got quite an imagination, that one." Rose was a nymphomaniac, he told me, who'd been unfaithful several times before. She was also an avid reader of porno magazines and most of the material in her tale was probably derived from there. He admitted to telling the children about the affair, *after* they'd asked why he and Rose were getting divorced, but claimed that they were already suspicious about their mother's behavior. After all, she had conducted loud phone sex with her lover, Diego, while the children were still awake and had once even masturbated where the children could hear her. In addition, according to Brady, the children had found love letters, lying around the house, that appeared to be written by Rose and that were clearly not intended for her husband.

Brady denied that he had ever been controlling in their marriage. "In fact, I spoiled the woman!" he exclaimed, which was actually somewhat consistent with Rose's description of the relationship. He told me he had never criticized her and that he had even had a tendency to put her on a pedestal because she was such a beautiful woman and had born him such wonderful children. He had always loved her very much and he still did, despite her idiosyncrasies and infidelity, and he would even be willing to take her back now, especially for the sake of the children. "Her parents, they're the ones behind all this," he grumbled. "Never did like me—especially her old man. No plumber could ever be good enough for *his* daughter." Brady declared that Rose's parents were now going to try and break him, financially. They were millionaires who could spend the next ten years in litigation. He, on the other hand, was only a simple plumber bordering on bankruptcy, he said.

I didn't like Brady at all. He struck me as sleazy and while he may have only been a "simple plumber," I also knew he made at least 1,000 dollars a week, mostly in cash, not declared as income. So why was he about to go bankrupt? He claimed he wanted custody of his kids, but he also implied that he'd be willing to let Rose have it if he could keep a certain condo they owned in Florida. Also, in the course of conversation, as we touched upon his alleged "kinkiness," he did admit to having once left a dildo in their neighbor's mailbox as a practical joke. He seemed to have no understanding of how this kind of behavior might be considered inappropriate or of the traumatic psychological impact this could have on a child who accidentally found the sex toy. But, it didn't really matter how much or how little I respected Brady as a human being. In the end, I still had two stories that completely contradicted one another and no way of knowing who was telling the truth. Unfortunately, I would have to leave justice aside for a moment and go purely with what was best for the kids.

Rose O'Connell had explained the origins of her affair to the children in this way: "So I went into the butcher shop and I looked at him and, you know, he looked at me, and voila!" Needless to say, this was not effective in gaining sympathy for her.

"I was dumbfounded!" cried Sean, during our initial one-on-one session. "How could she say that to me? How could she put it like that? 'Voila' and she sticks a knife in my father's back. 'Voila' and she destroys our lives!"

It would be a week later, though, in a joint session between Rose, Tim, Sean, and Casey, that I would really begin to see just how much the relationship between Rose and her children had eroded. Liz did not attend this session. She was a sweet, innocent nine-year-old who was having a lot of difficulty handling all this. Although she seemed to be somewhat in a state of denial, her weight had recently begun to balloon and I had decided that the less she knew about the conflict and the "affair," the better. Like her brothers, her school grades had suffered pretty drastically in the past few months, but of all the children, she also seemed the least upset with her mother and had indicated that she didn't mind living with her, provided that she did not have to split up from her brothers. Likewise, her brothers preferred not to split up from her, but, at the same time, would do anything to get out of their current situation.

The mood at the joint session was tense right from the start. As the four of them sat down in their chairs, Rose looked at her three sons, but none of them returned eye contact. I was somewhat amazed that they could live together, in the same house and yet could not make eye contact there in my office. The grievances began almost immediately. Mostly, they were verbalized by Sean. Tim and Casey both expressed a clear desire to move out and live with their father, but it was Sean, smarter and angrier, who was best able to articulate what was so horrible about Mom.

"She's unstable," he began. "She can't calm down for *two seconds*! She doesn't make me feel loved, she doesn't make *any* of us feel loved, and she takes everything with my Dad out on us, like it's our fault."

Rose leaned forward, stammering, trying to interject something, but Sean turned to her and, with a dramatic touch of over-enunciation, declared:

"We cannot handle you anymore."

Rose crumpled back into her seat, shaking her head. Then, she looked up at me and said, "It's not true. It's just … it isn't true! I was a great mother, Doctor." She turned to her sons. "Don't judge me on the few times I've messed up," she pleaded. "Think about who you can count on!"

Tim, who up until that point had been silent, opened his mouth and said, "We know who we can count on. We can count on Dad."

"We want to live with our father," added Casey.

Sean turned back to his mother and, his voice breaking, said, "You would need a heart the size of the Atlantic Ocean to make up for what you've done. You ruined my childhood."

Rose seemed at a loss. She turned to me, desperate, and told me, "They don't mean it. They don't mean it—they *love* me."

Finally, Sean turned to me and said, "Put it this way: If you were to offer me a million dollars to stay with my mom, I would thank you very much and tell you to keep the money."

That was it, that was all I needed to hear. The session was over.

I now understood what had to be done and it wasn't at all pleasant. I still didn't know who was telling the truth about the dissolution of the marriage, Rose or Brady. My instincts were that Brady was *at least* as guilty as Rose was, but it didn't matter. The children believed Brady and therefore, Rose was now going to have to be the "fall guy." I could try to make it seem like both parents were at fault, but inevitably, she would remain the wicked betrayer, while Brady would come out looking like the savior, and unfortunately it couldn't really be any other way.

Worst of all, even if Brady were to ever admit his role in Rose's infidelity, the children could never know about it. The trauma at learning that their father had coerced their mother into "perverse" sex games would be unbearable and could destroy them completely. Rose's version of the story, true or not, was a secret that would have to be taken to the grave.

My recommendations to the judge were as follows:

1. Physical and legal custody of all four children should be awarded to Mr. O'Connell, with liberal visitation for Mrs. O'Connell. Because, from the children's perspective, they had good reason to not want to live with their mother, they should not be forced to do so. While Mr. O'Connell had earlier claimed that he was on the verge of bankruptcy, the court had ultimately determined that he in fact had the financial resources to be the custodial parent and he agreed to reorganize his life and hire a full-time nanny, which I thought would be necessary. As Tim would soon be eighteen, he would have the authority to choose for himself where he wanted to live. He made it clear that he would live with his father.
2. Mr. and Mrs. O'Connell should be encouraged to tone down the rhetoric against one another. Mr. O'Connell should convey to the children that the reasons behind the divorce were more complex than they understood them to be and that they involved serious mistakes on the part of both parents. This way, the boys might begin to see their mother as less of a demon and it might prevent them from, as they grow older, blaming women in general. However, under no circumstances *whatsoever*, should anybody suggest that Mr. O'Connell was in any way involved with Mrs. O'Connell's affair. Also, both parents, especially Mr. O'Connell, should make every effort not to use their children as allies, messengers, or spies. The children must get back to focusing on their *own* lives, especially on school and peer relations.
3. Both Mr. and Mrs. O'Connell should take the children to psychotherapy to help deal with the impact of the divorce on their lives.
4. The children should never have access to this report. *Ever.*

Judge Anthony Costa, an older man with a conservative bent, began his decision by indicating that it was apparent why King Solomon's reputation as a wise man and effective judge was the result of a child custody case. He then proceeded to lay out a series of complaints he had against Mr. O'Connell. Mr. O'Connell was lacking in moral values, he said, and would thus be unable to instill proper values in the children. Additionally, Mr. O'Connell had indicated a lack of care for the children's psychological welfare by informing them of their mother's affair and encouraging them to spy on her. But, in keeping with my report, the judge did award Mr. O'Connell custody of Tim, Sean, and Casey—to be effective only when Mr. O'Connell set up proper accommodation.

The boys, the judge contended, had been brainwashed to the point that there was no real, workable choice but to put them with their father. Liz, on the other hand, was to remain with her mother. It would not be in her best interest, the judge said, for her to continue to use her brothers as role models, nor would it be advantageous for her to become, psychologically, a "fellow victim." While I certainly understood where Judge Costa was coming from, I thought this decision was ill advised. Not only was this not what any of the children wanted, but, furthermore, by splitting Elizabeth up from her brothers, the court was depriving her of a major source for emotional support. However, the judge had spoken and his decision was final.

It was a hard case, the kind I didn't like to think about very much. So, I didn't think about it much and, eventually, I had stopped thinking about it at all. But about two years later, I was entering the courthouse, on my way to testify regarding another case, when a woman called to me from behind.

"Dr. Marcus, is that you?" she asked.

I turned around, but the thin, pale woman standing before me was a stranger to my eyes. I stared at her, blankly, searching for any clue.

"It's me," she said. "*Rose O'Connell.*"

I squinted. Yes, it was Rose O'Connell, but she was barely recognizable. Once vibrant and beautiful, she now looked gaunt and hollow, brutalized. We spent the next twenty minutes or so catching up.

Her life was a living hell, she told me. Brady had never established a proper home for the children, nor had he followed up with any of the family therapy or provided the court with an honest accounting of his income, so all four children were still living with her. Tim, who had once been an "A" student, was now struggling to get by in a second-rate junior college. Sean and Casey were just barely passing in high school and still causing problems in the home, breaking rules and shouting excessively (in fact, the neighbors had called the cops on more than one occasion). Liz was doing all right in school, but had put on a lot of weight. While the children were now finally starting to warm up to Rose as a mother, this was only after a lot of fighting and heartache and they were still nearly impossible to deal with.

Brady, on the other hand, had troubles of his own and Rose was not the least bit sorry about it. The Internal Revenue Service (IRS) was starting to pay very careful attention to his cash business and other financial dealings. Meanwhile, he was still sweating out the judge's determination to make him pay everything he owed to his wife and children. The government had confiscated his passport so he wouldn't be able to flee to Ireland. In short, nobody had been spared, everybody was still suffering and the happy family that had once shared a home in Maspeth, Queens, and vacationed in Spanish islands was but a dim memory.

REFLECTIONS

In this tragic case, Brady's wish to make his wife have sex with another man moved from being a fantasy played out in the privacy of the marital bedroom to an enactment in real life. In the process, Rose's role as dutiful "love slave" took a twisted and unexpected turn, while their four children became entangled in the deterioration of the marriage. In the end, everyone felt betrayed.

It is often the case with the couples I see that there is a character flaw in one or both of the individuals that leads them to do something that has devastating, largely unintended consequences. In the case of the O'Connells, Brady's apparent midlife crisis, which ultimately propelled him to play out his perverse sexual fantasies beyond the marital bedroom, and his wife's capitulation to the "game," completely destroyed their marriage and family. Brady and Rose's lack of sound judgment and their consequent actions, combined with their putting their own needs (Brady's need for sexual gratification/power and Rose's almost obsessive need to please him) way ahead of their responsibilities to their children, were a lethal mix. When adults become parents—that is, *decent* parents—they must almost always put their children's needs ahead of their own. Giving, service, and sacrifice are the watchwords of good parenting.

By far the worst aspect of this case was that Brady told his children that their mother had cheated on him, thus casting her as the demon responsible for the family's demise. This was cruel to both his wife and children, though not surprising behavior for a selfish and infantile man like Brady. That Brady left out his decisive role in his wife's infidelity generates a measure of outrage that one can hardly stomach. Unfortunately, sadism, that "exquisite" pleasure of hurting someone else (frequently someone who has violated one's self-esteem and self-respect), often gets mobilized in hotly contested divorce/custody conflicts.

As in ancient Greek drama, the O'Connell's family situation was one in which betrayal was the predominant theme. Betrayal is a violation that cuts deeply into the wounded party, often irreparably. In this case, there were feelings of betrayal all around. Brady felt that his wife had betrayed him by falling in love with Diego, which was not part of the "game." The "turn on" of controlling and orchestrating his wife's liaisons was shattered by her actions, and he felt powerless and enraged. Rose, for her part, felt that her husband had betrayed her by pressuring her into these affairs, all the while reassuring her that everything would work out, and then, ultimately, telling the children that she was promiscuous. She felt abjectly deceived and humiliated.

Tim, Sean, and Casey felt betrayed by Rose's affair and by her discontinuing to act like the caring and responsible mother she had once been. Liz, sweeter and more fragile than her brothers, felt betrayed by both parents for taking away her stable and secure home environment. Finally, justice itself was betrayed, for it was impossible for me—or the judge—to determine with reasonable professional certainty whether Brady or Rose was telling the truth about the affairs.

Even if we could be certain which version of the story was true, the children clearly could not have been told. They had been told too much already and it had totally destroyed their affectionate feelings for their mother. If they had been told the full tale of their parents' perverse acting out, it would have shattered their positive feelings for both parents, irrevocably.

One can only hope that perhaps Brady might someday realize just how much damage his thoughtless actions inflicted and then attempt to make things a little bit better for his family. However, whether this does or doesn't happen, I will probably never know. Indeed, one of the most unsettling things about this line of work is that one rarely finds out what happens to a family after the judge's decision has been made—and whether or not one's recommendations proved to be, in both the long run and short run, really what was best for the children.

As a child custody evaluator, your decisions carry immense weight and responsibility and yet, at the same time, the tools you have at your disposal are limited and inadequate at best. Ironically, for this very reason, some evaluators might sometimes seem to take a light or even aloof attitude toward their cases. This should not be taken as a sign that they do not take their jobs seriously. Rather, on the contrary, it is simply due to the fact that if they were to constantly focus themselves on the extreme severity of their work—and on the consequences involved in getting it wrong—the emotional toll might be too much to bear.

CHAPTER 3

The Casals

"A proud man is always looking down on things and people; and, of course, as long as you're looking down, you can't see something that's above you."

—C.S. Lewis

When Aida Ramirez first arrived in the United States from Puerto Rico, at the age of eight, her father promised her, her two sisters, and their mother that America would hold a better life for their family. Six months later, he had abandoned all four of them. Aida went to school, got bad grades, and eventually, like her sisters, dropped out and took temporary jobs around the neighborhood. She was miserable and hopeless, but things began to look up when, at the age of sixteen, she met a young man named Hector Casals at a party in the South Bronx. Just three years older than she, Hector was short and mousy, but he had the confidence and attitude of a man twice his size. Within several months, Aida was pregnant with Hector's child and before the year was out, the two were married. Hector was tough, occasionally unfaithful, and sometimes even physically abusive, but Aida somehow managed to see past all this and the marriage was, if not thrilling, satisfactory.

Three years later, on a cold February night, Aida was sitting at home, watching her two young children, when she got the call. She had been staring at the clock, wondering where her husband was, when it came and she listened anxiously as the police officer on the other end of the line told her the bad news. Hector had been arrested for killing one man and seriously wounding another in a barroom brawl on Lincoln Avenue. Her husband had hit both men over the head with two wooden chairs, but these details were lost on Aida as she stared at her two toddlers, playing in the corner, and wondered what all this meant for the future of her family.

In a small, run-down courthouse on Grand Concourse, Hector Alberto Casals, who in the past decade had already been charged with drug dealing, attempted assault, and possession of an illegal weapon, was sentenced to fifteen to twenty-five years in prison and sent off to a maximum-security facility in rural New Jersey. From the little he could piece together, the place was a zoo and Hector was about to become the newest animal in the pen. He'd tough it out, he thought. He had survived as a youth on the mean streets of the South Bronx and he'd survive this too. Anyway, Aida would be there, waiting with open arms when he got out, a light at the end of a long, dark tunnel.

Aida Casals planned on staying faithful, really, she did. During the first three years of Hector's incarceration, she visited him regularly and there was no doubt in her mind that when he emerged from prison, they would be together again, as they'd been before. But when she began to realize just how long from now that would be, she started to have second thoughts. It wasn't exactly as though they'd been in the midst of a great marriage, she told herself. She could wind up waiting twenty-five years for an abusive, philandering husband, and a neglectful father who had barely been able to support his family (before his arrest, Hector had been out of work for months and had taken to drug-dealing in Jackson Heights to earn money). It was not long after these doubts had begun to set in that Aida met Nicolas, a tall and handsome immigrant from Argentina, who all-but-moved in with her and promised to marry her once she divorced Hector. For Aida, lonely, weary, and struggling to get by on public assistance, Nicolas was just what the doctor had ordered.

The old merry-go-round creaked as the October wind pushed two swings high into the air. Eight-year old Daniel Casals turned his attention back to the short, scruffy-looking man sitting on the opposite end of the seesaw. Daniel had just asked something a moment ago and now the man, who they told him was his father, was responding in his tough, raspy-sounding voice:

"Who told you that, your mother? She's just stupid. Nah, I didn't murder nobody."

It was five years since Daniel had last seen Hector. Now he and his younger sister, Lisa, would be spending two nights with him on a "trailer visit" (a visit in which family members can stay overnight at the prison) and the thought of this did not make Daniel feel comfortable.

"I didn't murder nobody," Hector repeated, eyeing his young son forcefully. "She's screwed up, your mother, messed up in the head, and it's all 'cause of that loser, Nicolas."

Nicolas was almost like a second father to Daniel, but he knew he wasn't about to tell that to Hector. The conversation turned to other matters, like softball, chewing gum, and school, but the words "stupid," "screwed up," and "loser" kept on echoing through Daniel's ears.

About a week later, Daniel lay awake in his bed in Belmont. He could hear the neighbors shouting at each other, as they did every night, but he was more disturbed by another noise, the barely audible sound of his mother crying in the next room. While Daniel couldn't know exactly what she was crying about, one thing was definite: she had to be talking to his father on the phone. Daniel guessed that they were probably talking about Lisa and him. After he and Lisa had returned from that first trailer visit last week, they had told their mother about the things Hector had said and that they didn't want to go back there again. Hector had responded harshly to this, saying if they weren't going to come back for a trailer visit, he didn't want them back at all, a reaction which confused and hurt Daniel. How could his father, someone who's supposed to love him, imply he wouldn't care if he never saw him again? It didn't seem to make any sense.

In the next room, Aida sighed as the voice on the other end of the line continued with its bitter, violent rant:

"Know what? Why wait 10 years? I got plenty friends on the outside, I'll tell one of *them* to fucking break his jaw. We'll see if you still wanna' marry him when his mouth is hangin' off of his face."

Aida tried to contain it, but she let out another sob—a small one, but clearly audible.

"Stop cryin'," her husband demanded from the other end of the line. "Stop cryin', you backstabbing whore, 'cause I'm the one who's gotta stay in here for twenty years and I ain't cryin'".

Enough of this, Aida thought, and she slammed down the phone and collapsed onto her bed. As she lay there, staring up at the ceiling and wiping away tears, the conversation played back in her head, including all of the many frightening threats against Nicolas. She knew Hector was probably full of hot air, but still, why did he have to be so vivid? She wondered if "backstabbing whore" might be a step up from "backstabbing bitch," the term he'd used in their last conversation. Had she really stabbed him in the back? Did she ever actually *promise* she'd wait fifteen to twenty-five years for him? She wasn't sure, that entire year was mostly a blur. But one thing she did know was that those kids were not going to be sent back on any more trailer visits, to hear about what a bitch she was, what a loser Nicolas was, and what an innocent angel their father was. She knew he was petitioning the court for more visits, but she also knew there were ways of preventing that from happening. There were legal options and she resolved to do whatever she could.

It was a Wednesday evening and I was about to dive into a large bowl of ravioli and marinara sauce when Tony, the law guardian, called me up with the info on this case. In many ways, it sounded typical. The children were having learning and behavioral problems and were currently enrolled in special-ed. The mother and father were fighting and not only over the children, but also over the formation of a new relationship. But the children's father being a convicted, imprisoned murderer—that was something I hadn't encountered in previous forensic work, and while it made the case more interesting, it also made it more disturbing. The return court date was scheduled for twenty-one days from now and so I finished dinner and immediately rearranged my schedule for the next few weeks.

In the next few days, I managed to interview Aida, Daniel, Lisa, and, last but not the least, Hector. Aida struck me as a decent, caring mother, who actually *was* trying to act in the best interests of her children. It seemed to me that she wasn't so much offended by her husband's badmouthing as much as she was worried about the emotional impact it might have on the kids. She definitely didn't want to take him out of their lives, but she was concerned about the potential effects of exposing them to his bad temper for such long periods of time.

She told me that the children were afraid of Hector and that they'd been afraid to tell her what he had said the last time, but, sensing something was wrong, she had managed to coax it out of them. Acknowledging her concerns, I suggested monthly, or maybe even bimonthly, visits and she seemed okay with the idea—provided Hector behaved himself and didn't trash her. The chances of that, she said, arching one eyebrow, were slim.

I felt sorry for Aida. Especially when she began to tell me about Nicolas, about what a wonderful guy he was, so different from Hector, about what a wonderful stepfather he would be. It was all a bit pathetic because it seemed fairly obvious to me that Nicolas had no intention of marrying her. He already had two other children (from a previous liaison) with whom he had no contact and it seemed to me that Nicolas was going to dump Aida the minute he sensed the slightest bit of responsibility rearing its ugly head. But, while I felt a powerful urge to explain all this to Aida, to let her know how naïve she was being, I held back. Nicolas, unlike Hector, wasn't any of my business and Aida wouldn't listen to my advice anyway.

Daniel and Lisa were interviewed separately, twice each. Daniel told me more about what his father had said about his mother. "She's married and what she's doing ain't right," he'd told him. He had explained to Daniel that Aida was only going with Nicolas for his money and he even told him some of the things he would do to Nicolas when he got out of prison (jaw-breaking included). Hector had also tried to portray himself as innocent of the crime, claiming that he had only acted in self-defense and that the man's death was mostly the result of poor hospital care. Daniel didn't believe any of this, telling me, "Bad enough you did it, you gotta' lie, too? He's gotta' think I'm stupid or something. If you're not guilty, why aren't you home, why are you in prison?"

Both children reported Hector having criticized their mother and Nicolas as being one of the primary reasons why they were upset with him. Lisa, a spunky little girl with lots of attitude, said if he ever did it again, she'd teach him a lesson and never speak to him again. Also, she reported that Hector had told her to "shut the fuck up" on the phone. But both children did admit that while the trailer visit was in many ways a frightening experience (especially the presence of police dogs and guards), it was also, at times, somewhat enjoyable. Lisa said she liked playing in the little playground and Daniel agreed that playing with his father and sister on the swings had been fun.

Four days later, I found myself staring at one of the most intimidating-looking buildings I'd ever seen in my life. The Sussex, New Jersey Correctional Facility, or "Sucky" as the inmates call it, is a long, rectangular building with an odd, triangular dome in the center, making the prison look almost castle-like. It is surrounded by rolling, green hills, and the contrast between the freedom and beauty of nature, and the dreariness of the prison was unsettling.

As I walked through the hot, brightly lit prison corridors, I found myself feeling increasingly anxious and depressed. Perhaps, it was the intense surveillance, or maybe it was the totally controlled environment, or perhaps it was the feeling of simmering anger and doom that permeated the place, but whatever the case, I knew I didn't want to stay very long. I had been told that Hector Casals, for the past few months, had been sinking into suicidal despair and now I was beginning to really understand. After being thoroughly searched, I was escorted into a small, chamber-like room and made to sit down on a rusty, metal folding chair. Several minutes later, Hector Casals was brought in and, as the guard watched from a square glass window, our interview began.

The first thing that struck me about Hector was his oddly blank expression. At times, he looked almost hollow, as if he wasn't really there, as if he were some kind of dummy. But then, he would suddenly become fierce and angry, and his eyes would come alive. I asked him about prison, about what it had been like so far, and he told me it was very rough, that he had gotten into some very serious fights, and that, in the past few weeks, he had even almost been raped. "Down here, you gotta' fight hard to get respect, cause' if they don't respect you, you're finished."

Then, his hardened exterior began to slightly give way as he described the loneliness, despair, and isolation of life on the inside. But he hoped to get out soon, he told me, adding that his lawyer was working very hard on getting his sentence reduced.

"That's wonderful," I said, remembering my meeting with his lawyer from the day before. Hellen Matthews, a pleasant young woman from the Jacobs and Stevenson firm, had told me that there was very little she could do for Hector and that he would probably be denied parole because of the many altercations he'd been involved in in prison. She also had repeatedly referred to him as "Hector Casaldo" and I could only hope she wasn't going to make the same mistake in court.

Hector's voice softened as he described his children to me, his "little prince" and his "little angel," whom he had seen only once in the past five years, but longed for every day. "They're the only thing that keeps me goin' in this hell hole. Without 'em, I'd find a way to check out," he said. He told me he hoped to have more trailer visits with them, once every three months, as allowed, and was working hard to keep up his good behavior, on which the visits were contingent. He didn't deny speaking badly about Aida, but said that it was largely because he felt she was distorting the facts, telling the children he was guilty when he wasn't. He explained to me that Aida was trying to ruin his relationship with the kids, because doing so would make things simpler and more convenient for her and Nicolas.

His rage at Aida was palpable: "I am her husband and I am their father and now, as I sit here, rotting in a cell, she's goin' on like I was never born, makin' a happy, new life and talking bad shit about me to my own kids." He told me that he resented Nicolas trying to act like a father to Daniel and Lisa and expressed serious concern that he might be attempting to discipline them. Leaning across the table, eyes burning with rage, he declared, "If I find out he's been puttin' his hands on my kids, there will be hell to pay when I get out. I'm gonna' beat his ass into a bloody pulp, you won't even recognize him, man, I swear." Out the corner of my eye, I glanced at the guard in the window, grateful for his presence.

As the interview came to a close, I explained to Hector that if he wanted the children to feel comfortable around him, it was absolutely essential he stop criticizing their mother. Gathering all of my courage, I told him that there was nothing to be gained from playing the blame game, that he needed to take responsibility for the state of his life, and that only then his relationship to his kids would improve. He seemed to understand, though I had my doubts he would be able to follow through. He was simply too impulsive.

When the interview ended, Hector showed absolutely no emotion, nor did he thank me for coming to see him. I explained to him once more that he couldn't badmouth Aida, and that if he did, he would screw himself over and probably not get another chance to make things right. I left, escorted by the guard.

As I walked through the corridors, steadily quickening my pace, I caught a glimpse, through a glass window, of the trailer playground. A strange image passed through my mind of Hector, with his blank-yet-fierce eyes and his bright, orange jumpsuit sitting on one end of the seesaw and the young and frail-looking Daniel sitting on the other. As I imagined Hector and Daniel moving up and down, up and down, I couldn't quite figure out if the image of father and son was touching and poignant or, instead, horribly disturbing. I walked on, passing through gate after gate until at last I had returned to the land of the free.

My recommendations to the judge were as follows:

1. Dad should have daytime, nontrailer visits with the kids—twice a month for the next three months and contingent upon his keeping his mouth shut about Mom. While the experience of visiting a parent in prison can be shocking and uncomfortable at first, if the visit is "talked through" in a sensitive manner by both the mother and father, children can adapt remarkably well, as the menacing external trappings give way to the positive aspect of building a relationship with one's parent. This, of course, would not happen, in this case, if either parent were badmouthing the other. I also recommended that Dad should have a mental health professional he could consult with and who could reinforce what he needed to do (and *not* do) to improve his relationship to the children. While this new arrangement could prove difficult for Aida because of the time and money involved in making the trips, it was a necessary sacrifice, which she would have to make.
2. It was a problem that the only means for verifying whether or not the father was behaving was from speaking with the kids, who, while nice kids, were absolutely unreliable in this regard. They could get confused and misrepresent things to their mother and, also, the situation allowed for the possibility that Mom could brainwash them into not wanting to see their father anymore. Therefore, if new problems arose and Aida once again contested visitation, I suggested coming back to me for a brief reevaluation.

The judge went along with my recommendations, with a few minor variations. Soon enough, Aida once again complained that she and Nicolas were being badmouthed by Hector and said that the kids no longer wanted to go see him. When push came to shove, she claimed that the kids absolutely *refused* to go, thus basically refusing, herself, to comply with the court order. As far as I know, the court did not continue to apply pressure on her or the children. Hector switched lawyers (reportedly, it took Ms. Matthews over half an hour to determine which of her clients was firing her) and, with the aid of the new lawyer, continued to look for ways his sentence might be reduced.

Seven years later, I ran into Tony, the law guardian, at Penn Station and I asked him what had happened to the Casals since the case had been closed. Tony had not heard very much, but said that as far as he knew, Aida and the kids were doing fine, now leading a new life with Nicolas acting as the stepfather. We bid farewell and as I sat on the train, riding home from the city, I once again saw the image of the brutal, angry Hector sitting on one end of the seesaw and the wide-eyed Daniel, sitting on the other, listening to what a "screwed-up whore" his mother was. Somehow, I doubted that everything was quite as hunky-dory as Tony had made it sound. When I returned home, I picked up the phone and, in the course of about an hour and a half, managed to track down Aida, and then, Hector's father. What I learned did not surprise me.

Several months after the birth of Aida and Nicolas' new baby girl, Nicolas ran off with another woman from the neighborhood, leaving Aida to raise and support the child herself. At the time of our conversation, Aida had not heard from Nicolas in over five years, but believed he was now living with the same woman in Jackson Heights.

Lisa, Aida's older daughter, had performed badly in elementary school and eventually dropped out of high school. Several months later, she became pregnant. Because it was unclear who the father was, Lisa had to take on three jobs to support the child.

Daniel, while initially a good, hardworking student, eventually let his grades slip and fell in with a bad crowd. A few months back, he'd been arrested for attempting to steal a car. He somehow managed to avoid prison time, but, nevertheless, his future did not look bright.

Hector had continued to get into fights in prison and had recently almost been killed. Like Ms. Matthews, Hector's second lawyer had completely lost interest in his case and it didn't look as though Hector would be emerging from prison any time soon. According to his father, "When they locked the boy up, they threw away the key." In seven years, neither Aida, nor any of the children, ever returned to see him.

REFLECTIONS

There is much to be learned from this sad story, especially from the self-destructiveness displayed by Hector. He suffered, above all else, from excessive pride—that haughty attitude shown by people who believe, usually unjustifiably, that they are better than everyone else. First, Hector was strikingly unwilling to take responsibility for his actions. Whether he was lying to himself or to his children about why he was in jail, whatever excuses he was coming up with, he was into the blame game. He was too proud to understand that he would be better off all around if he stopped playing the victim and simply told the truth—to himself, to his children, and to the parole board. This is what I tried to convey to him during our meeting in prison, to little avail.

Second, Hector was unable to control his rage toward his wife, rage which was most likely really rooted in his own dissatisfaction with where his life had taken him. His expectations that Aida wait for him were naive and unfair. Hector had been a lousy husband, abusive, unfaithful and neglectful, and still, unbelievably, he demanded Aida's loyalty. Mother Teresa herself would have had a hard time waiting for this guy to get out of jail.

Third and most importantly, instead of thinking more deeply and honestly about his own bad decisions and conduct, Hector kept insulting Aida and badmouthing her to the children. In part because he had a limited ability to reflect on his past, or imagine a realistic future, it hardly occurred to him that the kids might be totally allied with, and loyal to, their mother and that nothing he could do could change that. Every time he opened up his big mouth and criticized Aida to the kids, he was only hammering another nail into his own coffin. The kids never returned to visit him for he was simply an emotional burden they did not want, or need, to endure. As I told Hector at one point during our meeting, "Remember, words are like loaded pistols."

What was evident to me was that Hector had a necessity to see himself as hugely important and deserving of total loyalty from his family. However, this was, in his mind, based only on his position as husband and father, without any requirement on him to act in a responsible or caring manner. It was this sense of entitlement, without delivering anything remotely positive to those he claimed to love, that constituted his tumor of pride.

As for Aida, she was a well intentioned, though incredibly naïve, woman. She just could not see the forest for the trees when it came to the men she got involed with. Attractive and goodhearted, she had an incredible knack for choosing losers. Coming, herself, from a rough background, Aida just could not understand, let alone change, her pattern of going after exciting men who promised her the world and delivered nothing but disappointment, abandonment, and more kids to take care of.

With respect to the kids, it is sad but not surprising that they ended up the way they did. With a father who constantly put their mother down (sometimes in the most crude ways possible) and everything else that was dysfunctional in their overall family system, it is only natural that they eventually heeded the call of the street. Actually, their fates were almost entirely predictable. Lisa, after constantly hearing her mother described as a "whore" by her father, eventually became sexually promiscuous, herself, and wound up a teenaged mother. Daniel, for his part, became a criminal like his father. Looking for a sliver of anything positive in this story, I imagined that perhaps Daniel unconsciously yearned for some type of intimate connection with his father and figured he could perhaps be reunited with him in the same jail cell.

CHAPTER 4

The Stallones

"The injustice of it is almost perfect! The wrong people going hungry, the wrong people being loved, the wrong people dying!"
—John Osborne

Maria Carman stood on the sidewalk, waiting to cross, staring out blankly at the passing cars. Her thoughts were still on the conference. It seemed that her entire conception of the advertising industry had been off, maybe even way off, and that in 1995, it was almost as easy for a woman to rise to the top as it was for a man. The final two speakers had both been females and the second one, who spoke about market research, had looked like what Maria might in ten years from now. A trivial point maybe, but still somehow encouraging.

As she made her way across the street, Maria's mind drifted once again to that second speaker, to the way she had even *sounded* like Maria, and so she tragically never saw it coming. Weeks later, the driver of the bus would say that she had appeared out of nowhere and that there had been no time to slow down. This was probably true, though Maria would never be able to know for sure. The next few months would bring intense physical pain, combined with long, sleepless nights in hospital rooms, wondering why she couldn't think straight or remember the name of her mother's cat. Despite the presence of the best doctors and state-of-the-art treatments, recovery would be slow. But "recovery" is a very tricky word. For even many years later, when hospital rooms were but a distant memory and doctors' faces had all blurred into one, Maria Carman would look back and reflect that the young and talented career woman who had stepped out onto Bell Boulevard in Bayside, Queens, on that fateful January day, was long dead.

Officer Vincent Stallone skimmed through the half-torn magazine again, hoping maybe there was something interesting he'd somehow missed the first two times. There wasn't. He took another look around the waiting room, at the new faces that had entered in the past few minutes. There was now a man in a neck brace and Vincent wondered who between them was in more pain. It was an odd habit he'd picked up, ever since his fall from a broken paint ladder. Whenever he would see anyone with a neck injury, he couldn't help but think about whose injury was more severe, who was worse off. His eyes shifted from the man in the brace to a young woman, standing in the doorway, and suddenly it was as if the rest of the room had evaporated. The woman was Italian, like him, and she was perhaps the second or third most beautiful woman he had ever seen in his life—and that included photographs of Gwyneth Paltrow.

When she finally came in, the woman sat down in the only available seat, which, thankfully, happened to be the one right next to Vincent's. He immediately began to make small talk. In most ways, he was a shy and unassuming man, but for mysterious reasons, when it came to opportunities like this one, Vincent could suddenly become bold and confident. They talked about their accidents. She had been hit by a bus. Like him, she had been in and out of physical therapy for the past few months and, like him, she wanted more than anything just to get back on track, to feel valuable again, not like a patient. There was something sweet about her and something immediately likable. There was also, he detected, something ever so slightly off.

Something off. A couple of years later, Vincent would reflect on that first impression. He'd been perceptive—why couldn't he have been just a little more perceptive and ended it right there? Now, Captain Jackson was leaning in and explaining in a voice self-consciously helpless, "Understand, Vinny, we don't *want* to take your gun. But, you know, she keeps on calling and her allegations, well, they're ridiculous and no one believes 'em, and nobody *cares* what goes on in your home, anyway—but we've gotta' cover our asses, you know? It's just legal bullshit, that's all."

Bullshit was right. His eyes trained to the floor, Vincent slowly reached into his holster and took out the gun. Without looking up, he handed it to his captain, who nodded and hurried off. Vincent kept his eyes down—he knew for certain the other officers were staring. Fine, he thought. If it was a divorce she wanted, it was a divorce she would get.

Two years after their divorce and three years after the initial meeting between Vincent Stallone and Maria Carman, my own impression of Maria was a lot like Vincent's had been. She was beautiful, likable, and very sweet. And she was cooperative and responsible about keeping appointments, which, to a psychologist like myself, is just about the most important character trait a human being can have. But unlike Vincent, I did not get the impression that there was something "ever so slightly off" about Maria. I thought that she was *deeply* troubled. In her early dealings with me, I found her to be, by turns, immature, histrionic, excessively vulnerable, and heavily prone to confusing fantasy with reality.

She also seemed to have frequent difficulty controlling her behavior, especially when anger at her husband was involved. If I offered her a pencil to fill out forms, it was almost guaranteed to be broken in two by the end of the session. If I offered her a cup of coffee, there was a strong likelihood it would eventually be hurled at the wall in a moment of high frustration.

Of course, these kinds of symptoms were not entirely uncommon in the patients and clients I'd worked with in the past, especially those involved in child-custody disputes. Still, intuition, combined with years of professional experience, told me that I was dealing with something more than your average, run-of-the-mill behavioral disorder. A half-hour chat with Maria's neurophysiologist, Dr. Brill, confirmed my suspicions that Maria's problems were actually directly related to her accident. According to the doctor, the serious physical damage to Maria's brain had resulted in retrograde amnesia (the inability to remember certain events that occurred before the trauma) and a mild loss of intellectual capacity. More important, it had significantly worsened Maria's ability to modulate, inhibit, and control her own behavior.

Over the years, she had recovered impressively and had compensated for most of what was lost through hard work and therapy. But the damage was still there, still affecting her. It was exaggerating all of her least rational and most impulsive preaccident personality traits. And for the situation we were now in, that was very, very bad.

The situation we were in, like many I come across in this field, was basically a mess. Vincent, now two years divorced from Maria, was requesting liberal visitation with their two-year-old son, John. Maria, who had sole custody, had absolutely no intention of letting that "two-bit, Joel Steinberg for the 21st century" anywhere near her child, unwatched (he had previously been allowed only supervised visitation). He was a physical abuser, she said. If he were allowed that kind of time with John, he might kill him, just like he'd tried to kill her many times before. Vincent, for his part, seemed more than a little perplexed by these allegations and very hurt by his ex-wife's unwillingness to let him see his son in an unsupervised context. John was "the apple" of his eye, he said, the last thing he thought about each night and the first thing he thought about each morning. He denied ever having hit Maria or John, as she'd claimed he had, or having made threatening gestures with his gun, which she'd also claimed he had done. He conceded that, yeah, there had been a lot of yelling, and maybe even some mutual pushing and shoving, but no hitting—God-forbid! In other words, it was a classic case of he-said-she-said.

So, whom should I believe? Were Maria's claims, despite Vincent's persistent denials, nevertheless true? My initial feeling was that they were not. Vincent struck me as a fairly decent and balanced individual. Good-humored, mostly relaxed, and visibly concerned for the welfare of his child, it seemed that Vincent's biggest problem was *self*-destruction, not the destruction of others. Take, for example, his escape from his mother. By Maria's account, Vincent's mother, Harriet Stallone, was an extremely overbearing and domineering woman. She had smothered him, tried to control him, tried to keep him a child forever—and so it made perfect sense that he should want to marry the first girl he fell in love with.

What did *not* make sense was that this girl should wind up being Maria, someone so innately similar to Harriet. Maria and Harriet were not *exactly* the same, and they were different enough that they were still easily able to despise each other. But, in the way they related to Vincent, they were almost identical. In both relationships, Vincent wound up finding himself denigrated, dominated, and subjugated. Like his mother, Maria would grow resentful if Vincent ever tried to assert himself and finally, when John was born and Maria now had someone she could control completely and be completely adored by, she told Vincent goodbye.

Anyway, following up on Maria's claims about Vincent's volatile behavior, I did a bit of investigation at Vincent's place of work. Vincent's supervisor at the station, Captain Marvin Jackson, told me that Vincent was an all-around excellent officer who had never been cited for a single conduct violation and who displayed nothing but calm professionalism when he worked his beat in Bushwick, New York. Bushwick, for anyone not acquainted with it, is a neighborhood that is roughly as safe as 1980s Beirut. The captain's assessment came across to me as a major revelation. In contrast to Maria's claims, what Captain Jackson's description seemed to indicate was that Vincent was a man capable of maintaining control and acting responsibly in the kinds of environments where an impulsive, violence-prone person might easily be set off.

But the truth has a way of coming out and it was a letter I came across in the file written by Vincent and Maria's family physician, Dr. Mark White, which made me seriously rethink my perception of Vincent. The letter, written several years before, had stated, in no uncertain terms that Maria "had been abused and physically beaten by her husband." When I confronted

Vincent with the contents of this letter, he replied that Dr. White was on Maria's side and then went on to claim that the doctor had been a perverse homosexual who had spent more than thirty minutes examining Vincent's testicles (and had at one point during the examination informed Vincent that he was "getting hard").

Attempts to get in contact with Dr. White were unsuccessful, but I soon met a social worker named Jim Greenberg who had engaged the couple in marital therapy and also had alarming things to say about Vincent. Greenberg informed me that Vincent had actually admitted to hitting his wife and added that during at least one of the sessions, Maria had looked "pretty bruised." When I confronted Vincent about this, his response was more of the same. He denied any physical abuse and said, of Greenberg, "He's in her pocket, in her family's pocket." Why Vincent expected me to take his word over those of the doctor and social worker, I don't know. At any rate, it didn't happen.

Still, even though I no longer believed that Vincent had never hit his wife, I did not believe that Maria's characterization of him was quite accurate, either. Maybe Vincent had lost control, maybe he had even on occasion struck Maria, which would have been beyond inexcusable. But there was little evidence that he was the perpetually violent *monster* she was trying to paint him as.

Furthermore, there was evidence to suggest Vincent's abusive behavior was highly context-dependent. Meaning, when Vincent did lose control, it seemed it was usually in response to his wife's provocation, as opposed to an expression of a basic violent tendency. For instance, once, when I pressed Maria into giving me more details about a time Vincent had given her a black eye, she grudgingly admitted that she might have egged him on. What had she said to him? "Why don't you just go back to your mommy and fuck her hard like we both know you want to?"

Hmmm. Punching your wife in the face is certainly not the correct response to a suggestion like that. But the story didn't exactly make Maria look like a poor innocent victim either.

Maria was in fact quite prone to exaggeration and excess. When I asked her once for a chronology and some brief notes concerning her marriage, what I got back was a 175-page handwritten document informing me of everything from arguments she'd had with her mother-in-law over flowers to the way her husband's snoring sometimes kept her up at night (but sometimes didn't). By contrast, Vincent's document was only ten pages long.

When I asked Maria for her parents' home phone number, so I could arrange an interview, Maria became strangely paranoid. "My parents? My parents? What do they have to do with anything?" I carefully explained my reasons, but she kept on stalling, saying she didn't want to bother them, didn't want to stress them out—even though we had all agreed that their input was going to be integral in this process. Finally, she said, "I will give you their number, Dr. Marcus, but only on the condition that I'm present when you call."

"Mrs. Carman," I responded, trying to remain patient. "You are not in a position to dictate terms."

But she didn't accept that, could not accept that it was I, not her, who was in charge of this evaluation. We remained on the phone another forty-five minutes, with Maria ranting on about her "psychotic" husband and still refusing to give me the number.

When I finally did manage to get in touch with Salvatore and Ellen Carman, I began to second-guess just how much Maria's behavioral problems were actually the result of her accident. For instance, at one point, in the beginning of my in-office interview with Salvatore, he suddenly paused and asked, "Hey, how do I know that you're really Dr. Marcus?"

I pointed out that it would be highly improbable that an imposter would know so much about his daughter's marriage, wouldn't it? He hesitated, then nodded, but still insisted I show him my driver's license.

Salvatore's wife, Ellen, was similarly suspicious during our interview and even more so during a follow-up conversation on the telephone.

"Are you taping this call?" she'd asked.

"Of course not," I answered, and asked why she would suggest such a thing. "Well, you might want to try and use this conversation against my daughter."

As I reflected on what she had just said, on the downright *bizarreness* of the exchange, she added, "You know, you took a long time to return my call. A real fucking long time." I try to return phone calls as soon as possible so as to cause no inconvenience to my patients. But if a day and a half constitutes a "real fucking long time," then guilty as charged.

More odd than even that exchange was the phone message I found on my answering machine one night about a week later:

"Dr. Marcus, this is Channel 7 News. The world wants to know the facts on the Carman–Stallone case. Please call us back. We are *all* waiting."

No name, no number, but I immediately recognized the voice of Maria's brother, Frank, a construction worker in Queens. When I confronted him on the subject, he denied making the call and then asked me if I had been the one calling his home and hanging up at 2 A.M. every night.

"Of course not, " I answered. "Why the hell would I do that?"

"I don't know," he said, staring me squarely in the eyes. "I don't know *what's* going on with you."

It was then and there that the real truth finally solidified in my mind. That horrible bus accident in 1995 had done awful things to Maria's brain. It had tripped a lot of wires, had exacerbated some very troubled behavior. But there was a family pattern at work here. And in the end, the excessive paranoia, the need for absolute control, well, that wasn't the work of any accident. That was something in the blood.

My recommendations to the judge were as follows:

1. There is no evidence to suggest that Vincent Stallone represents a physical threat to his son, Jonathan. And while there is evidence to suggest a history of occasional physical violence by Mr. Stallone, it seems that under normal circumstances (unlike the present one of high tension and restricted supervised visitation) Mr. Stallone is capable of acting civilly toward his wife. Furthermore, he has demonstrated a dedication and love for his son as well as the prerequisite parenting skills to have liberal, unsupervised visitation—including overnights—with him.
2. To avoid overly upsetting Maria Carman, the liberal visitation should be implemented *slowly*. Furthermore, to aid in the transition, it would be beneficial if both parents received some degree of individual psychotherapy and parental guidance.
3. There is a strong possibility that Maria Carman will see her ex-husband's liberal, unsupervised visitation as completely unacceptable and will attempt to systematically interfere with it, perhaps through unsubstantiated abuse allegations, inappropriate use of police, extended litigation, etc. If that happens, she should be threatened with sanctions, including financial penalties, loss of custody, possible jail time, etc. A law guardian or parent coordinator should be appointed to supervise the infant's welfare and monitor the parents' cooperation with the court's orders. The situation should be handled delicately and extremely skillfully so that Ms. Carman does not panic and do something drastic.

Five years passed and the case slowly evolved in my mind from that of a sad story involving real people to a paycheck that was coming in the mail once a month. Vincent had owed me a lot of money and he had been paying it off monthly. When I did think about the actual case, it was with a certain sense of pride. There had been so many bad feelings and so many ambiguities, and complexities. But I had heard nothing from or about Vincent or Maria in a long time, and silence usually meant success.

Usually. It was on a January afternoon, probably not unlike the one that nearly killed Maria Carman, years before, that I received a telephone call from Vincent. There were several documents he needed from me for tax purposes, something to do with his payments. When he told me what had happened to his life in the time since we had last spoken, I was shocked, but somehow, not entirely surprised.

Vincent's first visitation with John had gone well. They had played together for several hours, reading Dr. Seuss books and making fake sandwiches out of play-doh. Maria had been present and was polite and cooperative with Vincent, even offering to make him a real sandwich. In all, it had been one of the happiest days Vincent could remember in a very long time. But when Vincent returned to their apartment two weeks later for his second scheduled visitation, he was surprised to find it empty. *Completely* empty. Maria and John had disappeared without a trace.

Years went by as Vincent devoted all of his energy and resources to finding Maria (the police were generally unhelpful, though he was able to utilize a few connections from the force). When he finally tracked her down, living in a small house in Michigan, it had taken nearly all his money and three private investigators to do so. Vincent, Maria, and a now four-year-old John appeared before a judge on a late Friday afternoon. Vincent's lawyer explained the situation and begged the judge to contact a New York judge and law guardian to verify that Maria had unlawfully fled with the child. He also demanded that Vincent be granted immediate possession of John. The request was denied and the judge postponed the hearing until after the weekend so that Maria could obtain a lawyer, as she'd requested. By the time Monday morning rolled around, Maria and John had vanished again.

Vincent, financially broke, never did find them a second time, though he managed to learn, through shadowy sources, that Maria had become part of a loosely connected network of women on the run and was being provided for by her family. Heartbroken and hopeless, the dream of reuniting with his little boy shattered, Vincent suffered a terrible nervous breakdown and had to retire from law enforcement. At the time of our phone conversation, he was trying to get his life back together, to get on with it. Most of all, what he wanted was to put the pain and sorrow behind him.

I wished him good luck.

REFLECTIONS

One of every parent's deepest terrors is that their child will be kidnapped, never to be seen again, and this fear became a tragic reality for Vincent Stallone. That his son was taken by his ex-wife makes his story that much more ironic and chilling. Maria, although she initially came across as sweet and likable, turned out to be something of a Greek siren—a beautiful woman with an alluring appeal who ultimately proved completely destructive.

By misjudging Maria's character and pathology, by not realizing, or even considering the fact that she and her family showed signs of genuine psychological problems, Vincent was emotionally sucked in deeper and deeper, until it was too late. Even friends had actually warned him that the relationship was a bad move, but he had ignored them.

This leads to an important lesson: Choosing a partner when one is "down and out" so to speak, emotionally vulnerable, and needy (such as when one is on the "rebound" or when one is ill) is never a smart move. Moreover, such decisions can be irreversible in terms of their negative, sometimes even *lethal* effects, as was the case with Vincent, who eventually lost his son.

The case of the Stallones also demonstrates clearly the limited capacity of the legal system to protect children and the rights of their parents. While in my report, I did not exactly suggest that Maria represented a flight risk, I did mention that the situation needed to be dealt with extremely skillfully, through a combination of law guardian, parent coordinator, therapist, etc, to ease the transition. None of this was implemented prior to the judge's decision to allow Vincent to have unsupervised visitation.

Maria was left feeling trapped and helpless, which ultimately led her to panic and flee with the child. Even worse, when Vincent finally located his son and Maria in Michigan, the judge did not properly and carefully consider the circumstance of the situation—that Maria had possibly kidnapped the child. Instead, he treated the case like any other custody/visitation dispute that could wait a few days. That it was late on a Friday afternoon and the judge wanted to finish for the weekend, and so did not bother to call the appropriate professionals in New York to learn the full story, is a tragic twist of fate that leaves one stunned, if not in tears.

It cannot be overemphasized that the legal system is made up of ordinary human beings who are flawed in their ability to properly react to and process situations, despite their best intentions. While our legal system tries to operate justly and mercifully, it cannot be relied upon to do the right thing, especially in unusual situations, like child custody/visitation, relocation, and similar conflicts.

CHAPTER 5

The Yangs

"Somewhere over the rainbow, way up high, there's a land that I heard of once in a lullaby."

—Yip Harburg

It didn't take long for Wei Yang to find a parking spot and that was a very good thing. At this particular moment in time, he didn't really have the patience to go scouring the lot and probably would have wound up parking in one of those reserved faculty spots and come to regret it later on. Fortunately, though, at 12:30 P.M. there were no other visitors to the school and he was able to pull in right in front of the main entrance. After a long, healthy drag off his Newport Lite, Wei stepped out of the car and briskly made his way up the cracked steps and into the John F. Kennedy Elementary School.

Once inside, Wei found himself standing amidst a giant swarm of students, noisily moving in every direction. Apparently, the bell had just rung, which, he realized, would afford him the opportunity to make this whole thing a bit easier or, at the very least, less humiliating. He might not have to talk to a teacher or administrator, or any adult at all. Instead, he could just try and find one of Steven or Michelle's friends, who would surely be as much help as anyone else.

Wei scanned the faces for anyone he recognized and came up short. He began to walk. To the students, this bald, smartly dressed, middle-aged Asian man must have looked like just another teacher. Perhaps, judging from his accelerated pace, a teacher late for his next class. Or maybe, judging from his anxious and determined expression, a teacher who had just found out which student had placed that thumbtack on his chair two periods before.

Wei turned a corner and then, suddenly, he stopped. Right there, only a few feet away from him, stood a boy he was sure he knew. But what was his name? The boy, definitely Taiwanese, had been over at the house a few times, he was a friend of Steven's and he'd be able to help. So what, Wei asked himself again, was the boy's name? Was it Matthew? No. Mitchell? No, but closer. Michael, perhaps? Yes! Yes, the boy's name was Mike, that was it, he was sure of it, and so now it was time to act.

Wei straightened up his shoulders and calmly made his way over to Mike, who was going through his locker, chatting with some friends. As he walked, Wei took in a deep breath, hoping, praying, that he'd be able to maintain a respectable composure for the duration of the conversation.

The boy recognized him right away.

"Hi, Mr. Yang!" he called out. His voice was cheerful, but you could tell by his face he was a bit perplexed to see his friend's father inexplicably roaming the halls of their school.

"Hello, Mike."

Wei looked at Mike's friends, who were now staring at him, expressionless. He looked back to Mike.

"Mike, could you please tell me, where is Steven?"

Mike squinted in confusion. Wei continued:

"Mike, I need to know where Steven is. And his sister, Michelle."

"I don't know what you mean, Mr. Yang. Don't you know where they are? I thought you were going with them."

"Going with them *where*?"

Mike turned silent. He now had a dumb, puzzled look on his face, which irritated Wei—which Wei actually felt like wiping off, to be matter of fact.

"Mike, I am not making a joke with you." he said, his voice firm.

"Mr. Yang, I don't know where they are!" the boy cried in frustration.

Could he be telling the truth? Was it possible? No, definitely not. Wei knew very well what children were like. They tell each other everything. A boy doesn't just pick up and leave town without sharing the upcoming adventure with at least a few of his comrades. Anyway, it was clear from the way the boy had clammed up when Wei asked where Steven had gone that he knew the answer well enough. He was just playing the fool, trying to help his friend, trying to keep his secret, *trying to ruin Wei's life*.

Wei began to approach, as several of the other kids stepped back.

"Mike, I'm going to ask you again . . . "

"Mr. Yang, I thought, I really . . . "

"Where the *hell* are my *kids*, dammit?!"

With this sudden outburst, Wei slammed the locker behind Mike with the side of his fist, causing Mike—and several others—to jump.

Wei stepped back and took another deep breath. His plans for remaining calm and composed had flown the coop. It occurred to him that if he didn't cool off right away, someone might run and get a teacher—if they hadn't already. He spoke again, his voice now soft, unthreatening.

"Mike," he began, "I didn't mean to frighten you. But please tell me, you must tell me, where are my children? As I'm sure you are aware, they have gone away, left me alone, and I need to know where they are."

About a thousand miles away, twelve-year-old Steven Yang stepped out onto the diving board and looked down. The water could not have been more than six feet below, but it felt like he was standing over the edge of a giant cliff. His reflection looked back up at him, its eyes begging him not to jump.

"Remember," they pleaded. "Remember the belly flop. Your stomach was red for *two whole* days. If you don't know how to dive, *don't dive!*"

"Shut up," Steven whispered under his breath. He crouched down for the liftoff, took several deep breaths, and then, to his utter amazement, completed a perfect dive, the first in his life. When his head finally rose to the surface, he could feel Michelle and Mr. Reid's impressed eyes upon him.

"Nice job!" Mr. Reid exclaimed, clapping. Mr. Reid, a tall, thin man with a bright white mustache, was their new next-door neighbor. He had lived in Jackonsville a decade, but had only built the pool two years ago. "Way too big for an old geezer like me to keep to himself," he'd said when he'd first invited Steven and Michelle to swim. Since then, they'd been spending time in the pool nearly every day.

Steven glanced over at Michelle. She was leaning back on the dragon float, sucking on the remains of a lemon popsicle and wearing those ridiculously large purple sunglasses. She nodded and smiled, acknowledging her brother's success.

Steven leaned back and eased into a back-float, squinting up at the clouds around the sun, averting his gaze from the sun, itself. He could hear the faint sound of a phone ringing from inside his house and the even fainter sound of his mother answering it. He ignored these auditory signposts of everyday life, however, and kept his eyes to the sky.

This was Paradise, he told himself and he knew it was true. This was every description of Heaven he'd ever heard and every Club Med commercial he'd ever seen. The only thing that was missing was a large group of scantily clad women feeding him bushels of grapes, and he felt like they might be arriving any minute. This was Paradise and this was going to be the rest of his life.

The sound of the screen door swinging open brought him back to reality.

"Kids!" his mother called out.

Steven shifted himself upright and looked to the house. His mother was standing in the doorway, a worried expression on her face.

"Could you please come inside?" she asked.

"What is it, Mom?" asked Michelle, lowering her glasses.

Before answering the question, Lien Yang glanced in the direction of Mr. Reid, who hadn't noticed her come outside. He was sitting on one of his lawn chairs with headphones on, leafing through a magazine that may or may not have been appropriate. Lien turned back to her children.

"Can you just come in? I need to talk to you in the house," she responded.

Several minutes later, sitting in their sunny, white, and turquoise kitchen, Lien broke the news to the children. They struggled hard to understand.

"But why?" demanded Michelle. "Why do we have to go?"

"It's . . . it's complicated," Lien responded. "But there's nothing we can do."

Unlike his sister, Steven remained silent. He was too busy reflecting on his new house and the new friends he'd made in the neighborhood—two of them even Asian! He thought about the swimming pool. He thought about the elementary school he'd gone to visit with his mother and sister a week and a half before, with its big white staircase out front and its colorful walls inside. He would now be leaving all of this and, worse than that, going back to New York City. Going *back to school* in Riverdale, where he had said goodbye to his friends for good and where they'd all been so jealous that he was moving to Florida, to the land of Disney World and Universal Studios (which, as it turned out, were far enough from his new home that he may as well have moved to Chicago). How could Steven now return and face everyone all over again?

He had a feeling he knew who was behind this and it wouldn't be that hard for everyone else to figure it out, too. Now, Steven's return to New York City would be the talk of the town, as would the entire mess taking place behind the scenes. *How could this be happening*, he wondered? And how could he return to New York and face Mike and Jessie, and that mean, fat Gary Woku? Steven looked back at the diving board. He wanted to jump off again. This time, though, he wasn't sure he wanted to come back up.

As a band played an especially schmaltzy rendition of The Four Seasons' "Sherry Baby," a tall, dark-haired woman offered my wife and me a plate of hor' douvres. It was my first fundraising event in a long time and I was grateful for the chance to relax. This was proving difficult, however, as I kept on running into colleagues who were somehow connected to cases I was working on. Among these friends and acquaintances was the venerable Judge Edith Wright.

I was in the middle of cutting myself a piece of cherry pie from the dessert table when Judge Wright spotted me and began her approach. As she came closer, the first thing that struck me was the dramatic incongruity between her storied personality and the fluffy, frilly, pink outfit she was wearing. Judge Wright was known as one of the hardest-hitting judges in the family court system. Over the years, countless tales had been told about her lack of sympathy or patience and her fierce defiance when it came to government or media pressure. Seeing her dressed up like Tinkerbell just didn't seem to fit.

"Marcus!" she exclaimed as she arrived. In the years I have known her, I have seldom heard her refer to anyone by anything other than their last name—at least not outside the courtroom, where formalities like "Mister" and "Doctor" are not mandated.

"Good evening, Judge Wright," I replied. I braced myself for yet another delightful conversation about work.

The judge shot a few quick glances this way and that. An off-the-record conversation between a judge and an evaluator at a social function is shady to begin with. If anyone were to overhear it, however, a clear line would be crossed.

"Marcus," she began again, her voice modulated to a loud whisper, "what the hell's going on with these Yang people?!"

"I don't really know yet," I replied. "I'm actually just getting started on it."

The Yangs were a case I had taken on about a week before. Judge Wright had been presiding over it for a few months now.

"I don't know what these people's deal is," she continued, "and between the two of us, Reynolds is screwing the whole thing up, royally. What was he thinking telling this woman to go to Florida? There was no half-decent reason to do that and Reynolds says 'go' because he feels like saying it, because he's a third-rate lawyer from a fourth-rate law school. I swear to you, I'm thinking about writing him up."

I wasn't sure how to respond to that. Andrew Reynolds was the lawyer for Lien Yang, the mother in the case. Lien had wanted very badly to move to Florida with her kids and Andrew had apparently encouraged her to do so even before it was clear that her husband, Wei, had given any clear consent. I agreed with Wright that Reynolds' actions had been problematic, but it hadn't occurred to me they might warrant serious disciplinary action.

Judge Wright continued:

"These people, these Yangs, I just don't know what they want. He's saying this, she's saying that, and it's all Chinese to me."

"Well," I replied, ignoring her off-color remark, "I'll try my best to sort it out. I've got a few interviews lined up for this week."

"Yeah, I hope you do. I hope you get to the bottom of this whole thing as soon as possible. Because let me tell you something, Marcus: If you don't clean this mess up *your* way, I'm going to have to clean it up *my* way. And *my* way's a lot less pleasant than *your* way."

Looking much like a thug in some Raymond Chandler novel, the judge downed the rest of her virgin Shirley Temple and walked off. This was not the first time I had been threatened by Judge Edith Wright and I had a feeling that, during the course of my career, it would not be the last.

Wei Yang, fifty, and Lien Yang, forty-two, had gotten married twenty years earlier in Lukang, Taiwan, in a marriage arranged by their parents. The marriage had actually almost died before it began, due to a dispute between their parents, but the matter was hastily resolved (not to anyone's entire satisfaction) and the wedding proceeded according to plan. Shortly after the wedding, the couple, along with their parents, moved to America, where they lived in New Jersey for several years before relocating to Riverdale, an uncharacteristically affluent section of the Bronx. Wei, a trained electrical engineer, opened a consulting business. Lien mostly stayed at home with the couple's two children, but sometimes worked part-time for a relative's carpet business.

The first twelve years of the marriage went quite smoothly and both Wei and Lien were mostly content in their new country. But as time went by and Lien began to grow more and more enchanted with American life, the couple's relationship began to unexpectedly shift. More and more, it seemed that while Lien was slowly transforming into an American woman, Wei was still living in Taiwan in his head. When Lien would pick up popular movies from the local *Blockbuster* and suggest that she and Wei watch them together, he would react with bewilderment. When she began to show more autonomy and independence than he was used to, he inwardly reflected that her speech and mannerisms were becoming more like the women one might see on an American television program than the respectful, traditional Taiwanese woman he had married (he was particularly shocked by an off-handed comment she made about possibly changing her name to "Linda").

But what pained Wei the most was not Lien's "Americanization," per se, but the fact that she no longer seemed to respect his authority in the same way she used to, even if she tried to pretend that she did. America had changed her, it was clear as day, and the discrepancy between Wei's expectations and the reality of Lien's behavior began to take a serious toll on their marriage.

If that weren't enough, adding to the strain were new tensions between Wei and Lien and their respective in-laws, all of whom lived in the neighborhood. The tension between Lien and her mother-in-law, Sun Lee, was especially strong. The two had never gotten along, but lately, Lien was finding

Sun Lee particularly critical and intrusive. Lien blamed her mother-in-law for butting in all the time and also blamed Wei for not having set appropriate boundaries with his parents. For instance, one time, when Wei and Lien were arguing, Sun Lee, who was sipping tea in the next room, suddenly chimed in, "Well, maybe if you showed a little more interest in him, he'd react how you'd like him to."

"What do you mean, 'more interest'?" Lien asked, visibly annoyed.

"You know. *In the bedroom.*"

What did she say? Lien was incensed. How could Wei have discussed such a personal aspect of their relationship, such a delicate and sensitive matter, with his mother? Wei, for his part, thought that Lien did not accord his mother sufficient respect and that it was Lien's parents, and not his, who were meddling in their marriage.

As their once-pleasant relationship began to tear apart at the seams, Wei and Lien started to realize that their marriage was coming to an end. Or was it? Neither was actually convinced, deep down, that it could not be salvaged, even if that clearly wasn't going to happen anytime soon. They were unhappy with each other right now, yes, but feelings change and who could say how either would feel in two years? Five years? *Ten years*? Should they actually get divorced? Or should they only legally separate? Neither was sure and this was not particularly surprising given the highly complex and now dysfunctional nature of their relationship.

One thing that had appealed to both of them, however, was the idea of picking up and leaving, and starting life anew someplace else. The couple had vacationed in Florida several years back and both felt that Florida would definitely be a better environment to live and raise their children in. Riverdale wasn't bad, but Lien longed to get out of the city, especially because she suffered from a respiratory illness (which she did not fully disclose, but which her doctor confirmed) and found the air in Florida easier to breath. Wei, for his part, preferred the slow and relaxed Floridian lifestyle to the hustle and bustle of New York City, even though his Riverdale business was doing quite well. If they did move to Florida, it was unclear whether they would live together or, in a more realistic scenario, Lien would live with the children and Wei would reside in another house close by.

Eventually, putting the Florida issue on the backburner, Wei and Lien concluded that their best option, for the time being, was to legally separate. Thus, Wei and Lien began the complex and acrimonious process of getting a separation. But as frustrated attempts to negotiate a fair financial settlement were beginning to stall, Lien suddenly and unexpectedly picked up the children and left for Florida, acting on the advice of her attorney. A furious Wei went to court and, a month later, Lien and the children had been forced to return to New York by an order of the judge.

Soon after Lien's return, Wei showed up at the house to discuss the matter with her face to face. How did Lien think she could just pick up the kids and leave without his permission, he wanted to know.

But he *did* give her his consent, Lien insisted. They had discussed moving to Florida many times, it was all part of their shared plan for the future!

Was it part of the plan, he wondered, for her to make off with the children without even telling him she was going, leaving him behind in New York, all by himself?

The heated debate devolved into a shouting match until Wei, a man of little patience to begin with, finally lost it completely and pushed Lien against the wall and slapped her across the face, hard enough to cause bleeding. Days later, she had successfully obtained an order of protection, which wasn't very difficult, as the couple's young son, Steven, had witnessed the entire incident.

Meanwhile, Steven and his sister, Michelle, absolutely refused to return to their Riverdale school and opted to stay home, instead. They just *couldn't* go back, they insisted, not for anything in the world. It was bad enough that they had bragged to everyone about moving to Florida and were now being forced to return, but when they learned that their father had actually *come to the school* and intimidated their friends into revealing their whereabouts, it was all just too embarrassing to live down. Roy Stewart, their next door neighbor in the Bronx, told them they were the talk of the whole school! Steven and Michelle thus resolved to never set foot in there again.

To sum up, the situation, when I entered the picture, had hit rock bottom. In Judge Wright's words, it was a "mess" and yes, I most certainly wanted to sort it out my way before she got the chance to sort it out her way.

I decided to interview the kids first. Steven, thirteen, and Michelle, ten, had been described by at least one teacher as "wonderful, happy kids and terrific students." I have no doubt that this was probably an accurate description of them as they had been several months before, prior to their move to—and return from—Florida. But those sweet and cheerful children had vanished and the Steven and Michelle Yang who entered my office, several days after my encounter with Judge Wright, were moody, bitter, and depressed.

Michelle, who I spoke to first, stared down at the floor as I struggled to get her to communicate with me. I had the sense there was that which she wanted to say, but that she was either too angry or too afraid to say it.

"I only want to help you," I stressed. "But I can't if you won't say anything to me. I'm going to ask you again to tell me about your father. It can be anything you like."

"I hate him," she finally said, eyes still on the floor.

"Why do you hate him?" I asked.

"Because he's a liar," she answered, this time looking up and establishing eye contact. "He told us we could go to Florida and then he said we had to come back!"

"He told you you could go?" I asked. That would definitely be a revelation.

"Yeah!" she answered. "Sure he did!"

"When did he tell you you could go to Florida?" I asked.

"I dunno', we talked about it all the time!" she answered.

"Can you give me a specific example?" I asked. "Did he know exactly when you were going to leave?"

"It's like I said, we talked about it all the time!" she replied, looking frustrated by the question.

I decided not to pursue that particular topic with her further. Whether or not Lien had left for Florida with her husband's knowledge and consent was still a very murky issue, despite Judge Wright's convictions that she definitely hadn't. But I did not think I would get a final answer from Michelle and wanted to focus on some more immediate issues.

"Did you always hate your father?" I asked.

Michelle hesitated.

"I dunno'," she said. "Maybe, but I never knew him that well. But I for sure hate him now, I know that much."

My conversation with Steven, who was several years older, was more illuminating. Though I was already beginning to get this picture from my meeting with Michelle, Steven confirmed that Wei had always been mostly absent from their lives, a figurehead more than anything else. He said that life for the past few years had been pretty much unbearable, as both children had had to endure listening to their parents yell at each other all the time. However, I got the impression that what bothered Steven the most was not the dissolution of his parents' marriage, but rather, the way in which it was dissolving on such a public scale.

"You don't understand," he told me, after being asked why he hadn't returned to school even though he'd been home for some time. "I can't go back there. I'm famous now. He turned me into a celebrity."

"You've got to go back to school eventually," I countered. "You're going to lose the whole year and you don't want to do that, trust me."

"No, what I *don't* want to do is go back. I can't! I can't deal with people looking at me, talking about me. And anyway, I've been gone so long now, so it's like too late to come back now, it would be too weird, right?" He closed his eyes and shook his head. "God, I just can't believe he did this to us," he muttered. "He's ruining our lives, you know that?"

"So, if you don't plan on going back to school, what do you plan on doing? Making a career of watching Jerry Springer?"

I thought my Jerry Springer line was rather witty (no such career exists!), but alas! Steven didn't even change his expression.

"We're going back to Florida," he said, firm and resolute. "Otherwise, I'll lose my mind, I swear it."

As Steven continued to describe his despair at the thought of staying in Riverdale and his heartfelt longing to return to the Sunshine State, something began to trouble me. All right, Florida was warm, beautiful, and relaxing— but would life over there really be that much better than it was in New York? After all, his father, according to the plan, would eventually be joining them there, too, and even living nearby. The friction between his parents would still remain a major part of Steven's day-to-day life.

I pointed this out to Steven and he responded that he was not trying to es- cape his parents' crumbling marriage, only the public scrutiny from friends and community members. But there was a problem with this answer. As Steven was no doubt aware, Jacksonville, the Florida town to which he and his family would be moving, was a very close-knit community, one which would surely be no less interested in the goings-on of the Yang family than his cur- rent community in New York. Also, Steven would no doubt have new friends who would all eventually learn about his parents' separation one way or an- other. In other words, the only really substantial differences between Florida and New York would be better weather and more elderly people.

And there was another thing that kept nagging at me. Steven and Michelle seemed to feel an intense animosity toward their father, but after listening to their descriptions of him, I just couldn't figure out what was so horrible or irredeemable about the guy. I believed Steven that his father was cold and withdrawn and I understood that it must have been intensely traumatic and enraging to witness him physically assault Steven's mother, even if it was an isolated incident and uncharacteristic of Wei's general behavior. But he still didn't sound like the complete monster that the two children were try- ing to describe. Out of everything, they seemed to view his forcing their re- turn to New York as his most heinous crime, the height of human evil, but I had a feeling his actions had probably been justified. I decided to press Steven further on the source of his hatred for Wei by asking a fairly routine question.

"Steven," I began. "Could you please share with me your father's four worst qualities?"

"Sure," he responded and thought for a moment. "Well, number one, he's cold. He doesn't show us *any* affection."

"Cold, no affection," I repeated, jotting the words down on my pad. "And number two?"

"Number two, he's like totally uninvolved in our lives. Like, he doesn't really seem interested in what we do."

"So, you mean, he doesn't come to school plays, little league games, that sort of thing?"

"Well, no, he does come to that stuff, but it's like he doesn't really care when he's there."

I nodded and wrote that down as well, wondering if this was really substantially different from answer number one. "And number three?" I asked.

Steven furrowed his brow.

"Well, he's ... he, you know—number three?"

"That's what I'm asking for."

"Well, he hit my Mom. Hit her *hard*."

"Yes, but you said that was a one-time thing. You told me he didn't usually get angry around the house. I'm looking more for general qualities, Steven— things that have always bothered you about him."

"Yeah," he said, shutting his eyes to concentrate. He was looking very frustrated.

"What's the third worst thing about your father?" I asked.

"He's—I dunno', he's really ... "

Steven looked absolutely helpless as he sat there, stuttering, and so I told him it was all right, that he'd told me enough, which he had.

I now understood the true nature of Steven and Michelle's desire to go to Florida and could see that it was not a *rational* desire (which is why it didn't matter that most of their problems were obviously going to follow them there). At the end of the day, for these two children, Florida was not Florida—Florida was actually a *dream*. It was a magical place where they could escape and live happily ever after, as all good children deserved to do. Yes, there were many legitimate and even compelling reasons to go to Florida and the place was, in fact, wonderful for all the reasons they stated, but ultimately, it wasn't Florida they were truly after. It was Utopia.

And just as Florida had morphed within their minds from an actual place into an idealized fantasy version of itself, the children's image of their father had undergone a transformation of its own. He was no longer just their father, the strict emotionally withholding man who paid for their meals. He was the object preventing them from going to Paradise. Wei had been simplified and reduced into the *obstacle*, the *antagonist*, the Devil, himself. It was a shame, but it was a situation that Wei Yang had partially brought upon himself, as I discovered when I interviewed him several days later.

Wei struck me like a deer caught in the headlights, a man who's carefully constructed life had suddenly come crashing down all around him and stunned him to the core. He knew that his relationship with his wife had been falling apart, had known it for a long time, but now it seemed he had lost complete control of his family. He had always worked so hard, dedicated his life, in fact, to providing for them. Now they were turning on him in the cruelest way possible—by acting like he didn't exist.

"I do not deserve this, Dr. Marcus," he told me, as he sat in my office, looking agitated. "I always did the best a man could do—the very best."

Wei continued to describe how hard he had worked, the sacrifices he had made, and I believed he was sincere in his claims that he had tried to be a good father and do right by his family. But I also thought that by being a cold and disassociated parent, he had forfeited the kind of emotional connection that might have prevented his children from being able to demonize him so quickly the moment something went wrong. Perhaps, Wei's detachment was rooted in his culture, perhaps it was just a function of his personality, or maybe it was a combination of *both* of these things—but whatever the case, for the American-bred Steven and Michelle, Lien was the only true parent they had ever known. This was made abundantly clear when I met her for the first time, a few hours after meeting with her husband.

Lien struck me as a devoted mother, extremely close with her children and, at least on the surface, dedicated to their best interests. I also got the impression that she still had not really let go of her positive feelings for Wei, even as she desperately wanted to break free from what she perceived as a restrictive Taiwanese lifestyle. On the issue of getting a divorce, she, like her husband, seemed hesitant to make a real decision.

However, not wanting a divorce right away was one of very few things the couple agreed on and as my interviews with both parents (conducted separately) continued, I soon found myself scrambling through the familiar tangled web of accusations and contradictions. Wei, for instance, was still adamant that his wife had left for Florida without giving any advance notice. Lien, meanwhile, maintained that Wei had granted his express verbal permission and, as our talks continued, I began to get the impression that the truth lay somewhere in between these opposing claims. It was clear that Wei and Lien had indeed discussed the possibility of moving the family to Florida (a draft agreement sent to me by their former mediator confirmed this), but it seemed that no specific date had been set and that when Lien, fed up with the lengthy separation process, took her lawyer's advice and decided to pack up and move, she did not notify her husband of the decision first. Whether or not she was completely unaware that Wei would be against the move remains unclear, but the fact that she left without calling him suggests that she was consciously leaving on the fly for fear of being stopped.

The couple also disagreed on several other important points. Wei claimed, for instance, that while he might support the family moving to Florida *eventually*, it was becoming increasingly clear that now was not a good time. Even if he joined them, he said, and lived in a separate residence, he would not be able to support them at their current standard of living and within six months, the family's savings would dry out and Lien and the kids would have to get used to a much more modest kind of lifestyle. Lien, he claimed, had not carefully considered the financial ramifications of the relocation and the fact that Wei would probably be forced to take a new job that paid only about half of what he was earning in New York. The Florida fantasy would therefore eventually implode for lack of funds.

Lien, however, told me that if Wei could not find as good a job in Florida, his properties and investments would be able to keep the family afloat at their current financial level for some time. She also indicated that Wei possessed more money than he was admitting to and that he would easily be able to find good work in Florida, unless he intentionally avoided doing so in order to force the family back North.

Not knowing whom to believe, I consulted a representative from Florida's association of electrical engineers and discovered, once again, that the truth lay in the middle. This gentleman informed me that it would in fact be substantially more difficult for Wei to obtain a comparable job in Florida within his particular specialty. However, it would by no means be impossible. The representative also reminded me that the cost of living in Florida was lower than it was in New York.

As I rummaged through all of the feelings, opinions, and facts I was being given to work with (the school system in Jacksonville was roughly equal to Riverdale's, I learned), the situation began to seriously deteriorate. Lien informed me that Steven and Michelle had begun to develop worrying signs of stress. They'd taken to eating less and engaging to various degrees in self-destructive behavior. For instance, Lien had returned from the grocery store one evening to find Michelle banging her head against her bedroom wall and crying. Steven had become silent and reclusive, hardly ever leaving his room, and had at one point made a casual comment about how he wished he could "just run away," which had terrified his mother, even after he assured her that he had not meant it literally.

I decided that the situation had to be dealt with immediately and devoted myself full-time to the completion of the report. I estimated that I could probably finish it in about ten days if I were given maximum cooperation from all parties. To finish it so soon would be a very difficult task, though, and would mean putting everything else in my life on hold, focusing very hard, and, frankly, even risking the quality of the report. Normally, I like to spend at least two or three months on any given evaluation. The less time an evaluator devotes to a given case, the more likely it is that he or she will misconstrue what is really going on and/or be fooled by one or more of the parents. Usually, it is only over time that the various parties' actual motivations emerge, giving a more solid basis for the evaluator to make conclusions. However, in regard to this particular case, where the children had already deteriorated so much and were beginning to self-destruct, time was of the essence. I simply could not afford to wait for illusive revelations to emerge at their own leisure.

My recommendations to the judge were as follows:

1. Physical and legal custody should go to the mother. All of my interviews (including those with Wei) had indicated that Lien had been an excellent, hands-on parent who was regarded by her children as dedicated, loving, and responsible. While she had no doubt complicated their lives unnecessarily by taking them to Florida without the legal authority to do so, this did not negate the fact that she had been a good mother and had raised her children well. Wei, on the other hand, had managed to completely alienate them and so deciding who should get custody was pretty much a no-brainer.
2. The children and mother should relocate to Florida, after which a liberal visitation schedule with the father should be worked out, using a mediator in Jacksonville that I would choose for them. This visitation schedule could not be worked out *before* the move, because the real-life circumstances of the parents and children in Florida had yet to be determined (presumably, Wei would move to Florida as well and live separately).

   (I was not under any illusions that through these visitations, father and children would bond and become the best of friends. However, I believed that once the relocation had taken place, with time, Wei and his children would at least return to their previous emotional set point.)

I was not entirely satisfied with the conclusions presented by my report and felt that the father, who was being forced to leave his business, was on some level getting the short end of the stick. But at the same time, this seemed the only truly sensible solution. After all, both parents had revealed an essential desire to move to Florida eventually—they only differed on the timing and circumstances. The way I saw it, three out of four members of the family wanted to move to Florida immediately and only one did not. I just did not see why

Wei's desires should be placed ahead of everyone else's, even if that meant he would have to make certain substantial sacrifices. On top of that, the move to Florida would likely help in healing the relationship between the children and their father. Furthermore, it seemed that the children's basic quality of life and that of their custodial parent, Lien, would ultimately be enhanced by the move to Florida.

(As a side note, I had also briefly considered recommending that the children remain in New York, but change schools or neighborhoods to avoid scrutiny and "shame." But the children were dead set against this and I did not think it would be in anyone's interest to force them to do it. Plus, I considered Lien's well-documented respiratory problem a legitimate reason to get out of New York altogether, if that's what she wanted to do.)

I was not present at the emergency hearing that was held shortly after the judge received my report. However, from what I was told by the law guardian, it was no less messy and tension-filled than the case, itself. Judge Wright was particularly furious that the children had not returned to school all the time they'd been back in New York, despite a clear court directive to do so. How had the parents let this happen? Who did these people think they were?

Eventually, according to my source, the judge called the lawyers for both parties into her chambers.

"Listen up," she said. "You've got till 4 P.M. to settle this case. Relocation, separation, the whole kit and kaboodle. If it's not settled by then, both Mom and Pop are going to jail for contempt. I don't give a shit what anyone else thinks. I ordered them to send their kids to school. Poor babies didn't want to go? Tell me, who the hell does? This is a courtroom, people, this is the law—live with it. All right? 4 P.M."

Now this might sound like a rough and unconventional approach and it most certainly is. But in situations like this, where the parents are deadlocked and the children are suffering, judges sometimes have to go to extremes and play hardball if they're going to make headway with the case. For this case, it worked like a charm.

The lawyers, upon being presented with the ultimatum, went into a frenzy, as did the parents, and by 3:50 P.M., the case had still not been settled. But by four, with court officers standing by ready to spring into action, an agreement had finally been reached. Lien and the children would move to Florida immediately, with Wei's full consent. The financial agreement would mirror the one they had previously been negotiating with their mediator, though Lien would compromise by accepting a lower amount of child support in exchange for the right to relocate. The judge approved the settlement and arrangements for the move were set into motion.

A year and a half later, Wei had moved to Florida, as well, and was living less than a mile from Lien and the kids. The family's funds had not dried up, though Wei was making less money than he'd been making in New York (it was still a good job). Wei and Lien had not divorced, mainly because Wei still clung to the dream of one day reconciling with her and transforming her back into the woman she used to be, the one he had once fallen in love with, long ago. Lien, though, had grown less and less interested in returning to Wei and had little interest in marriage in general. She was working as a schoolteacher in Jacksonville and loving her new, southern lifestyle.

The children, meanwhile, were flourishing, though their relationship with their father was still cool at best. Michelle had achieved the highest grades in her new class and Steven had made it onto his school's swim team. In general, it seems that the children have finally returned to their normal, happy state. But appearances can be deceiving. Traumatic childhood experiences, like the painful circumstances and humiliation that nearly brought Steven and Michelle to the brink of self-destruction, can be swept under the rug, even forgotten, but that doesn't mean they don't leave a mark. And whether or not the children are aware of it, there can be little doubt that the period of darkness they endured will remain a part of them forever.

REFLECTIONS

Relocation disputes are amongst the most difficult kinds of cases for judges and evaluators to decide. This is in large part because the reasons that a parent gives for wanting to relocate are usually fairly sensible and in many ways in the best interests of the children. For example, in our case, Lien Yang wanted to relocate to Florida in part because she had respiratory problems and the Florida air would be healthier for her and also, more importantly, because the children had never really been happy in Riverdale and Florida seemed to offer them a genuinely better life. Wei, himself, believed that Florida would be a better place for the family to live.

That being said, even when the grounds for relocating are sensible, there are often very good reasons not to do so, as well. When relocation takes place, somebody often has to suffer because of it and it's usually the parent who was left behind, the *noncustodial parent*. If they do not follow the rest of the family to their new location, this parent will inevitably have a very different and most likely inferior relationship with the children from what they used to have when the whole family lived in the same area.

Even visitation will only help so much, as in such cases, it can be very unwieldy for everyone involved and tends to become harder and harder as the children get older. Teenagers are particularly difficult to maintain long-term visitation schedules with because they tend to be deeply enmeshed in their peer groups, schools, and communities. For a teenager, the idea of getting on an airplane or taking a long road trip to go and see Dad is something that gets less appealing as time goes by. As a result, the relationship between the teenager and his or her noncustodial parent becomes strained, if not seriously degraded.

It is also worth mentioning that relocations are often driven by the custodial parent wanting to consolidate a relationship with another partner—a stepfather or stepmother for example. Thus, the process can make the noncustodial parent feel marginalized, if not displaced and replaced. This, of course, then leads to acrimony between the parents, with the children caught in the crossfire.

Sometimes, as in the case of the Yangs, bad legal advice can lead a custodial parent to relocate without the permission of the court and/or the noncustodial parent. This kind of situation creates absolute havoc for the children, especially if the court then orders them to return, disrupting their lives yet again. In the case of the Yangs, while Mrs. Yang did not *permanently* relocate without permission, she did the next worst thing—she relocated and made it seem to the children that it was a "done deal," and that they would be staying in the Sunshine State forever, even though the relocation had not been properly authorized.

Fortunately for the children, the judge in this particular case felt it was ultimately in their best interests to remain in Florida and strong-armed the parents into settling the dispute in a fairly reasonable manner. Still, it must not be forgotten that the relocation struggle between Mr. and Mrs. Yang, and their unwieldy way of dealing with one another and the children during the dispute, led to Steven and Michelle's lives being radically disturbed and further alienated them from their father. These kinds of disruptions and damaged relationships can often have severely negative long-term impacts on children's ability to maintain an inner sense of security and optimism as they move through the various stages of their lives.

CHAPTER 6

The Lopezes

"We lie loudest when we lie to ourselves."

—Eric Hoffer

It was almost 11:30 P.M. and I was up late, going over some notes in my home office, when my work line rang. Despite the hour, this was not particularly unusual, as people often leave late-night messages on my machine, expecting me to hear them in the morning. I leaned over and answered the phone.

"Hello?" I said.

There was silence on the line.

"Hello?" I repeated.

"Dr. Marcus?"

The voice was harsh and gruff—one I did not immediately recognize.

"Yes?"

"When you write your little report, don't be talking shit about Ms. Gonzalez. Shit we both know ain't true."

I leaned forward to get a better look at the caller ID. Predictably, it read: "Caller Unavailable."

"Who is this?" I asked.

"Don't worry about me, Doc. Just worry about yourself."

Click!

As I sat there with the phone in my hand, the open line humming out of the receiver, my mind raced. Should I star-69 it? No, the call had been blocked. I leaned back in my seat and took a deep breath. It was late enough as it was, but now I was going to have to try and fall asleep with *this* on my mind. I thought back to what had brought me into this whole situation. It had all begun with a thirteen-year-old girl named Melody Lopez. . . .

Nearly every classroom in America has a Melody Lopez, a child who is simply not on the same page as everyone else. A kid who's a little bit strange, dresses a little bit funny and who nobody wants to talk to and, more importantly, *be seen* talking to. When Melody wasn't around, the other children would tell stories about her, about how she always radiated the faint odor of cheap cigarettes, about how her mother, that "whore" from 161st Street, didn't let her take showers except on the weekends. Sometimes, either through somebody's negligence or somebody's cruelty, these tales would find their way back to Melody. She didn't mind though—or at least she told herself that enough times that it almost made it so.

Some of what they were saying was probably true, anyway. She didn't take a lot of showers. Mom always said it was a waste of water. What was she supposed to do, fight with her about it? Like *that* would do any good. The last time Mom had conceded in an argument was probably before Melody was born. Better to ignore what the other kids said—kids will always talk about you—that's just what they do.

Melody didn't really care what people said, it didn't bother her all that much, and that's what made her earrings idea all the more absurd. Where had that stupid idea come from, she wondered, and then she remembered. She'd been sitting in class, struggling to pay attention to Mrs. Jordan's lecture, when her eyes had wandered over to Stacey Cole's earrings.

Stacey Cole was what you might call the "It" girl, the girl with the nicest clothes and the nicest hair and the one who all the boys stared at during class and then tried to talk to during recess. Right now, Stacey was wearing pink and silver diamond-shaped earrings and it occurred to Melody that her mother had earrings just like them. Melody couldn't help but wonder what would happen if she, herself, were to show up to school wearing earrings like those. Was it possible that it might just ever-so-slightly alter people's perceptions of her? Melody cautiously considered the possibility. Sure, she wouldn't turn into Stacey Cole overnight, but, at the very least, the earrings might boost her confidence, and maybe people would treat her a little bit more like *someone*. It was a stupid idea—*so* stupid—and like most stupid ideas, though she couldn't know this at the time, it would lead to nothing but trouble.

When Melody got home from school that day, Mom wasn't home yet. Melody's mother was assistant manager for Quacks, a local 99-cent store, and she often wasn't around when Melody got in. Melody didn't mind, though. It was much easier to relax without Mom and her boyfriends in the house, who were always arguing about this or that.

As she sank down onto the sofa and picked up the TV remote, Melody suddenly remembered about the earrings. She sighed. There was no way in hell Mom was going to let her borrow them, she realized. And, of course, she couldn't take them without asking—that was out of the question. Maybe, though, if she really begged Mom and promised to do extra chores or spend a few nights of the week at Grandma's (thus giving Mom some private time with Julio), then Mom *might* do her this one favor.

Melody wondered if the earrings really were just like Stacey's. She hoped they were a little bit different—otherwise, people would say she was just copying Stacey. She turned off the TV. Surely, there'd be no harm in just taking a look in Mom's drawer to see what the earrings looked like, provided the door wasn't locked. Melody put down the remote and went upstairs.

As Melody turned the doorknob to her mother's room, she felt a twinge of guilt. Then, she remembered all the times she had come back to her own room to discover that comic books or magazines had been thrown out because Mom didn't like them cluttering space—and the guilt quickly drifted away. Melody opened the door and stepped inside.

The drawer where Mom kept most of her less expensive jewelry was located in a chest in the corner of the room. Melody walked over to it, bent down, and opened it up. The earrings were there and they were heart-shaped, not diamond, but it was something else that caught Melody's eye. At the side of the drawer, only inches away from the earrings, were four small plastic bags containing what looked like sugar. Melody was only thirteen, but she was old enough to know, with quite certainty, that the white powder in the bag was *not* sugar.

At that very moment, Carmen Maria Gonzales—Melody's mother—stepped into the open room, almost as though she had materialized from thin air. Melody hadn't heard her come into the house! Carmen's eyes widened in what appeared to be horror or anger, or some combination of the two.

"Melody, what the *fuck* are you *doing* in here?!" she exploded.

"I was just—I was. . . . "

But Melody couldn't complete the sentence and Carmen rushed over to her, slammed the drawer shut, and pulled Melody to her feet by the collar of her shirt. She leaned down so her face was right next to Melody's.

"Listen to me, Mel. You didn't see, nothin'. Got it?"

Melody nodded, and Carmen pushed her out of the room and closed the door behind her.

Over the next few days, Mom didn't bring up the incident and Melody put it out of her head—along with any secret ambitions for achieving classroom popularity. But then, about three days later, the subject came up again when Carmen was dropping Melody off for her court-ordered weekly visitation with her father. As Carmen and Melody were entering the lobby, Carmen suddenly stopped, placed her hand on Melody's shoulder and gripped it firmly—so firmly that her nails dug in a little, causing Melody to wince with pain.

"Mel, I got something important to tell you."

Melody looked up at her mother. Carmen's face was tight, tense. Whatever this was, it wasn't going to be pleasant.

"I talked to Julio last night. I mentioned, you know, what happened the other day and, well, he was very angry. *Mucho enfadado.*"

Carmen was right to assume that it hadn't taken Melody more than a few seconds to figure out who the cocaine in her mother's drawer had belonged to. Carmen never made any effort to hide her misbehavior from Melody, so there was no question for Melody that Carmen wasn't secretly dealing crack. Julio Santana, on the other hand, was well known around the neighborhood as a drug dealer and all around thug. He was also Carmen's latest boyfriend and inarguably her most violent companion yet. On several occasions, Melody's mother had returned home from a night on the town with a black eye or a bloodied lip and one night Melody had even witnessed Julio throw her mother against a wall in their very house. And then there was that day when Melody hadn't seen Julio do what he did, but she had seen the *results* well enough. Melody didn't like to think about that day.

"I tried to reason with him, Mel," Carmen continued. "But you know how Julio gets. When he's pissed off about something, ain't nothin' gettin' in his way. You're not going to tell your daddy about what you found, right?"

"No," Melody answered.

"That's good. I was worried...." Her voice trailed off and then she leaned in closer to Melody.

"Mel, you tell anyone about this, you tell your daddy or the court...Julio says he's gonna' *kill* you. And your daddy. Gonna' kill you both!"

Melody's eyes widened a little bit, but she didn't say anything. What was there to say? Melody understood Carmen and Julio's paranoia. Carmen's custody of her was shaky at best—always was—and all of them knew that Felix Lopez, Melody's father, had recently hired a pretty good custody lawyer to contest it. The drugs in her drawer would not bode well for Carmen's case. More important than that, Melody suspected, was the jail time they could buy Julio when the police traced them back to him, which wouldn't be hard.

But Melody also knew something else. She knew that if she told her father about the drugs and Julio's threat, Julio would never find out—not unless her father *wanted* him to. In other words, telling her father could only be a good thing. He would understand the dangers as well as she and he would know better than her what to do and would act accordingly. So, Melody, when she arrived at her father's apartment on the fourth floor, chose to tell him everything. About a week later, to her infinite delight, Melody had been removed from her mother's house and into her father's apartment after he was granted temporary legal and physical custody of Melody on an "emergency basis."

Not surprisingly, here and now is where I come into the story. When I received the call about the case, Melody had been living with her father for two and a half weeks and her mother was vigorously fighting the custody transfer (and her humiliating one hour a week of supervised visitation). She was also fighting the serious abuse and neglect allegations that were now pouring forth from Melody and Felix's lawyer, allegations that Carmen never would have dreamed she'd have to face. Had the world gone mad, she wondered? Melody's allegations weren't backed up by a single shred of evidence or proof—how could the court be taking them seriously? And how could Melody, the child she had raised and cared for for thirteen years, suddenly turn on her like this, like an ungrateful wretch? It was beyond belief!

For my part, I was supposed to render an expert opinion based on Melody's best interests both in terms of custody and visitation. From what I knew of the case, it seemed that the two sides were in total disagreement. Melody and her father were claiming that Carmen had been a downright awful mother who had seriously neglected and psychologically abused Melody. Carmen, however, was accusing Felix of brainwashing Melody in a clever scheme to avoid having to pay child support for her (instead, Felix would be able to *receive* it from Carmen).

To get the bottom of it all, or at least to somewhere *close* to the truth, I decided to interview Melody first. The impression I got of Melody, when she came to my office in Queens, was that of an articulate, appealing young girl who was in great pain (how she was articulate and appealing if I described her previously as a social outcast who was "a bit strange" is something I'll get to later). Melody described life under her mother as a continuously harrowing experience. A particular source of anxiety, it seemed, was the volatile and destructive boyfriends that Carmen had a strong tendency for getting herself involved with.

It seemed that for each of Carmen's boyfriends, there was at least one awful memory associated with him. For instance, there was Enrique, a tall, mustachioed Dominican whom Carmen had been with two years before. Enrique could sometimes be friendly, but there was a smarmy, slimy quality to him, like anything he said had to be taken with a slight grain of salt. One time, Melody was awoken in the middle of the night by her mother, who seemed utterly panic stricken. Enrique hadn't been answering his cell phone for hours, Carmen told her. She was sure he was cheating on her—she just *knew* it, she said. Carmen then forced Melody to get up and help her roam the streets, looking for him. They didn't find him and by 2 A.M., Carmen decided to call it a night. The next morning, over breakfast, Carmen informed Melody that she had finally reached Enrique's cell phone at four o'clock in the morning—and a strange woman had answered!

"What do you think of *that*, Mel?" Carmen asked her. Melody wasn't sure how to respond. Needless to say, the whole experience was far too miserable and uncomfortable for an average eleven-year-old to have to deal with like that and it made Melody feel awful.

Then there was Mauricio, a short, plump Puerto-Rican who barely spoke and once smacked Melody on the back of her head for turning the channel from a Yankees game she didn't realize he was watching. Melody didn't like Mauricio to begin with, but her feelings soured irreversibly when he deliberately ran over the family cat after a heated argument with Carmen.

The scariest of all of them, however—-the man whom Melody would frequently have nightmares about, was Julio Santana. Julio Santana was feared throughout the neighborhood as a man with a propensity for brutal violence and a criminal record that could make your average, local hoodlum swoon with envy. What Carmen saw in Julio was beyond Melody, especially after that time Julio did something *really bad* to her.

Melody had been visiting at her father's place and, at the end of the day, when her mother arrived to pick her up, there were thick strips of gauze attached to her head. Carmen didn't say anything about the gauze—or anything else—during the ride back. But when Melody returned home, she was confronted with a sight she would never forget: streaks of blood running down the white dining room walls. When Melody pressed her about what happened, Carmen claimed that she had tripped trying to replace a windowpane. But Melody could tell she didn't expect her to believe it—and Melody *didn't* believe it, not for a second.

Carmen's bad boyfriends, though, did not nearly represent the sum total of the problem. Carmen, when you got right down to it, was an extremely neglectful mother. She often left Melody alone in the house for many hours at a time, forcing her to look after herself, which often meant cooking her own meals. Also, sometimes Melody would wake up in the middle of the night to find the house empty, having no idea where her mother had gone or when she would be back. On top of all that, Carmen was also deceitful and, in recent weeks, had on several occasions outright lied to the court or significantly distorted things Melody had said to her.

For instance, Carmen had told the court that at a sleepover at her father's house, Melody had witnessed Felix engage in a drunken, homosexual orgy. This story had apparently *evolved* out of Melody telling her mother that her father had let an old high school friend sleep on the couch because the man had been too drunk to drive home. There was also no evidence that Felix was a homosexual, as Carmen claimed he was, though for the purposes of my investigation, it didn't really matter if he was. The personal sexual behavior of Melody's parents was only relevant when it seemed to have an adverse affect on Melody. And on that score, Carmen seemed far more guilty than Felix—at least according to what I was hearing from Melody.

According to Melody, Julio had sometimes encouraged Melody to lie in bed with him and Carmen, which, when she complied, made her feel "extremely uncomfortable." There was, it should be noted, no evidence that Melody had ever witnessed Carmen and Julio having sex or that Melody had ever been outright sexually abused by anyone. But Julio had once jokingly kissed Melody on the mouth, clearly against Melody's wishes, and in the presence of Carmen, who did nothing to intervene.

What upset Melody the most, however, seemed not to be her mother's bad behavior. Melody had a very clear-eyed view of her mother and understood that she was an extremely flawed human being and thus made many mistakes. But what she could not tolerate was the way her mother never admitted any of these mistakes, never owned up to doing anything wrong. The way Melody saw it, Carmen was in a constant state of denial, both about her own performance as a mother and about the way she was treated by the men in her life.

Melody's most recent visit with her mother had been particularly painful. Carmen had brought a gift with her, a book of games and puzzles, but no sooner had Melody thanked her and begun to look at it when the accusations started to pile on. Carmen sat down in a red chair across from her daughter and in a quiet, but emotionally charged voice, asked, "Why?"

"Why what?" Melody asked, putting the book down onto the table and getting ready for what she knew was coming.

"Why are you doing this?" Carmen answered. "Why are you telling these lies? What has that man done to my poor baby to turn her into a monster like this?"

"He hasn't done anything to me, Mom," Melody replied.

"Come on, Mel. We both know what kind of a mother I was. We both know how happy you were with me."

"Happy?" Melody asked, her blood beginning to boil. "*When* was I happy? And if I was, how would you even know about it? Most of the time you weren't even around!"

"There you go again," Carmen responded with a knowing smile. "Making up stories. If I wasn't around, who took care of you all the time? Who made dinner for you?"

"Who do you *think*?" Melody shot back. "Who do you think made dinner for me when you were out all night hanging around with your boyfriends? I did!"

"Come on, now, Mel. You know I made dinner every night. Enough with the lies, they're breaking my heart."

"What are you *talking* about?" Melody cried, totally exasperated.

"Tell me, how did he do this to you?" Carmen asked, leaning forward. "How did your father turn my little girl into some kind of devil I don't even recognize? When are you gonna' stop being his puppet, Mel? He doesn't love you and he never did. You know that!"

Melody had had enough and felt it was now her own turn to ask the questions.

"Why do you stay with him, Mom?"

"With who?"

"With Julio."

"Julio? I love Julio. And he loves me."

Melody shook her head. "I saw what he did to you that time, Mom. We both know you never tripped hanging a windowpane."

Carmen's eyes suddenly widened and she looked like she was about to slap Melody across the face, but then she noticed the supervisor and must have thought better of it. She turned to the supervisor and gave a little smile, the kind that said, *Kids really do say the darndest things, don't they?* Then, she got up to leave.

"I'm gonna' leave now, but I want you to think about what you're doing," she said as she opened the door of the room. "You're destroying our family."

Most other sessions weren't much better. According to Melody, much of the time, Carmen would continuously denigrate Felix, talk about how she never should have hooked up with that "fag" (Melody had been conceived as the result of a casual affair between the two, who were never married) and would make sly references to what might happen if Julio got too angry. Melody described herself as "pooped" after each session. Incredibly enough, though, she still loved her mother and did not request to terminate the meetings. Yes, she had done her wrong—was *doing* her wrong—but Carmen was still her mother, the woman who had given birth to her and Melody still had *some* positive feelings for her left.

That all changed very soon. One day, about a week into my evaluation, an unwanted visitor arrived at the front door of Felix Lopez's Mott Haven apartment. No, it was not Julio, who had been avoiding the spotlight rather scrupulously since Melody's custody transfer. Instead, it was Don McKenzie from the Administration for Children's Services (or ACS). The ACS had received a phone call from a neighbor named Susan Eaton who had claimed that she had observed Felix sexually abusing Melody and watching pornographic films with her.

While the ACS would eventually dismiss the case (there was no "Susan Eaton" in the building or even on the block and the report was completely unfounded), Melody was forced to go to the hospital and undergo a humiliating, invasive, and extremely stressful gynecological examination in order to prove conclusively that she had not been abused and clear her father's name.

Now Melody no longer wanted to go on any visitations with her mother, who, it seemed pretty obvious, had actually been the one responsible for the abuse report. "Why should I go and sit in the same room with someone who makes me sick?" Melody asked. She hoped to push off all visitations until after the court case was over—and then, after that, she only wanted to see her mother for one hour a week with supervision.

Melody's official position on both of her parents, it seemed to me, was abundantly clear. Now, it was time to hear what *they* had to say.

Felix Lopez, at our first interview, informed me he had actually wished to wrest custody from Carmen for some time now. A few years earlier, he had become concerned by the way Carmen was entertaining a wide variety of disreputable men and so he had filed for custody. But his lawyer soon advised him that he would not be able to prove neglect and was, for the time being, better off accepting the liberal visitation agreement that was already in place. There were also financial ramifications involved. Felix worked as a licensed practical nurse in a small Manhattan hospital and was unsure he was really capable of supporting a daughter, full-time.

However, in recent months his situation had improved and with Melody's situation seeming to deteriorate, he now felt it was no longer a matter of choice anymore. Felix Lopez struck me as a decent man and a caring father, a stark contrast to the manipulative liar Melody's mother would paint him as in our first meeting a few days later.

Carmen Gonzales was an articulate, well-spoken woman who had lived in this country for two decades. Carmen basically repeated to me the same thing she'd told the court—that Felix had brainwashed Melody in an attempt to gain custody of her and thus avoid having to pay any child support (which, she said, would be more expensive for him than supporting the girl, himself). Melody was extremely vulnerable, she told me, and so she had been an easy target for her father's manipulations. All of Melody's life she had longed for his attention and now, suddenly, she was getting it in spades.

Carmen was very charming and she made her points in an earnest, convincing way. She denied all of Melody's claims and stories and made her own damning accusations about Felix. However, most of what she said sounded either suspect or, at best, was unsubstantiated. For instance, Carmen claimed that Felix had been an absentee father for most of Melody's life. But it was clear that Melody had been visiting her father consistently for at least a number of years and the mantle in Felix's house displayed numerous photographs of himself with Melody at various different ages. As for Carmen's repeated claims that Felix had exposed Melody to homosexual orgies and had been generally sexually promiscuous in her presence, there was no evidence to support this and the things she told me differed suspiciously in their details from what she'd told the court, suggesting one very ripe imagination.

Carmen's most important claim, of course, was that Felix had brainwashed Melody into lying about her. While I could not make any definitive determination as to the veracity of Melody's accusations (that was for the court to do), I could state with a high degree of professional certainty that Melody did not appear to be brainwashed or under the influence of her father. She spoke fluidly and descriptively when we talked and never seemed evasive in her answers. Also, she would often remember more details in the middle of a session and, in general, never seemed like she had been rehearsed or tested beforehand.

Most importantly, the accounts of friends and neighbors were much more in line with Melody and Felix's version of things than with Carmen's, indicating that if any brainwashing had taken place, it had more likely been Carmen brainwashing *herself*. She seemed to have created a fantasy life of the perfect mother–daughter relationship and seemed to have actually come to believe in it.

But the reality was very different.

Carmen's own mother, Celia, described her daughter as a self-destructive personality whose compulsive attachment to abusive men had inevitably prevented her from taking proper care of Melody. She said that Melody once told her she felt like she was "living in a prison" whenever Carmen's boyfriends were around. Lucy, Celia's other daughter and Melody's aunt, echoed her mothers' sentiments and stated that her sister should receive extensive "psychological help" before being allowed to retake her place as a prominent figure in Melody's life—and that she should *never* be allowed to regain custody. These were illuminating words coming from close family members, especially considering that, from all indications, Carmen had a fairly good relationship with her family.

A conversation with Valerie Jordan, Melody's seventh-grade teacher, provided me with an even clearer picture of the situation. Mrs. Jordan described to me how Melody, under her mother's care, had been the class outcast, a shy girl with low self-esteem who usually appeared unkempt, often wearing the same clothes for several days in a row, and who put little effort into her studies. Mrs. Jordan had been very concerned about Melody and so she had called Melody's mother, but Carmen refused to come in to discuss the matter and never showed up for any of the designated parent-teacher conferences. Finally, after Melody had received her report card on the last day of the Fall semester, Carmen called Mrs. Jordan and starting screaming at her, accusing her of trying to destroy Melody's future, until Mrs. Jordan eventually hung up on her. On top of that, Leonard Marx, the Catholic school's executive director, informed me that Carmen had failed to meet her financial obligations to the school and that Felix had had to step in and pay the rest.

Felix, unlike Carmen, had attended parent-teacher conferences and had impressed Mrs. Jordan as attentive and concerned. Furthermore, Mrs. Jordan said that from the time Melody started living with him, she'd become like a new person. She was always clean and well dressed and had become much more outgoing and self-confident (and her grades had improved significantly, as well). Mrs. Jordan told me that in all her years as a public school teacher, she had never seen a child undergo such a dramatic transformation in so short a time.

These interviews were important and provided a solid backbone to my report. But ultimately, they were secondary confirmations of what I could already tell simply by observing Felix and Melody interact in the waiting room of my office. As the two of them joked and giggled with each other, looking at magazines and picture books, it was clear that this was a father and daughter who were very fond and respectful of one another. It was also clear what both of them truly wanted and it was likewise clear what I would recommend to the judge.

It was at this point, as I was getting ready to draft my report, that I received the mysterious late-night call. I use the word "mysterious" very loosely, for it was no more a mystery that the caller was actually Julio Santana than it was a mystery that Felix's "neighbor," "Susan Eaton," had really been Carmen Gonzales. Julio's threat was certainly unpleasant, but it was going to do nothing to deter me from making my recommendations.

In virtually all occupations related to the Law, you are bound to sometimes make people very unhappy and threats and intimidation are going to be a natural part of the job.

I knew that Julio Santana was a dangerous man. But I also knew that he was a frightened man (the threat he made was itself proof of that) and he was not about to do anything to get himself into any more hot water than he was already in. Most importantly, I knew that if I was going to let anonymous threats control the way I conducted my evaluations, then I might as well close the book on my career right then and there. I decided, in fact, to include the threat in my evaluation because it underscored very nicely what kind of malignant forces the mother had let into her house for her daughter to be exposed to and thus highlighted how deeply distorted the mother's account of her wonderful home environment really was.

My recommendations to the judge were as follows:

1. Physical and legal custody should be awarded to Melody's father. As far as I could tell, Felix Lopez was a very adequate parent and from what I could gather from testimonials, Melody had been much happier and healthier under his care.
2. Melody should have supervised visitation with her mother for the next two years. However, these visitations should not begin until after a three-month period in which Melody has no imposed contact with her mother whatsoever.

   (At the time of the evaluation, Melody was sure her mother was responsible for the sexual abuse allegations against Felix and was furious that she had set up a situation that lead Melody to have to endure such an intrusive and humiliating exam (not to mention the embarrassment it brought on her father). She did not want to see her mother at all and I did not see any reason to force her to do so. When the visitations did begin, I recommended that they be implemented slowly and with much caution.)
3. Carmen Lopez should be mandated to have counseling at least once a week by a qualified mental health professional. The focus of these sessions should be on Carmen's parenting skills and her tendency to enter into abusive relationships, which hampered her abilities as a mother—even if Carmen still denied that she *had* such tendencies. I also suggested that she enter into a spousal–partner abuse program run by the state's Victim Services division.
4. Melody should enter into psychotherapy. Her mother, however, should not be present at these therapy sessions. I believed that Carmen's involvement, at this point, could only be harmful and that she should become a

participant only if and when she admitted to her neglectful and abusive behavior—and if Melody did not object to her presence.

5. An order of protection should be granted to Melody and her father against Julio Santana.

6. The contents of this report should remain absolutely sealed.

(Several parties were concerned about the potential for Julio to react violently if he were to find out what was said about him—and by *whom*.)

In the end, the judge affirmed most of my recommendations. Melody remained with Felix and did not see her mother for several months. She also entered into therapy, as per my recommendation, and Carmen was ordered to do so, as well. When I was last updated on the case, about a year and a half after the trial, Melody and her mother had still not reconciled and there had only been a few, scattered visitations between them. Carmen had never entered into psychotherapy, herself, despite the court's orders that she do so, and she had never followed through on the spouse–partner abuse program she was supposed to participate in. Most importantly, she never took responsibility for her failure to be a proper mother to Melody and still maintained that her daughter had been brainwashed into making false accusations and that their lives together had actually been wonderful.

Melody's social life and grades continued to improve and eventually flourish and, according to her psychologist, she was doing very well in her therapy, which he planned on terminating soon. Of course, only time will tell what the long-term effects of her difficult childhood will have on her. My guess— my *hope*—is that this gentle and intelligent girl will have a good chance at a good life. I would only be lying to myself, however, if I thought that the pain she had been forced to experience in her early life would ever truly be healed.

As for Julio Santana, despite his violent reputation, he never made good on any of his threats—either to me or to Melody or her father. Soon enough, he was out of the picture, anyway. About eight months after the trial ended, Carmen finally left him for a man named Michael Salgado. Carmen reportedly told friends and family that she had finally found her soul mate in Michael, a tall, charming "businessman" from the neighborhood who had recently spent seven years in jail for armed assault.

REFLECTIONS

It is often stated that the lie about a misdeed is often worse than the misdeed itself.

In the case of Carmen, it seems pretty clear that what hurt Melody the most was not her radically flawed parenting (the neglect, the exposure to the horrible boyfriends, etc) but rather her absolute refusal to *own up* to any of it. It might be unfair to call Carmen a "liar," though, at least in the traditional sense, for it seems that she was not necessarily intending to *deceive*, but rather, was, herself, in a state of denial. It was this self-deception that allowed her to protect her own self-respect and self-esteem, while still maintaining her pleasure-seeking lifestyle. Carmen wanted to believe she was a great mother because it left her guilt-free and she went to extraordinary lengths to convince herself of this lie, inflicting further damage on Melody in the process.

However, the real truth was fairly obvious, especially in light of Carmen's outrageous allegations to ACS and the court that Felix was sexually abusing Melody, which forced Melody to undergo an invasive and unnecessary medical examination. Carmen may have actually on some level believed that Felix had abused their daughter, however she caused Melody to have to go through a humiliating and frightening experience with no thought or concern as to how this would impact on her. For this, Melody would never forgive her.

Another phenomenon this case highlights, in addition to parental neglect and denial, is the use of intimidation, which is so common in so many custody disputes. The examples of intimidation being employed in this story are many: Carmen tried to intimidate Melody into not saying anything about the cocaine by telling her that Julio would kill her and her beloved father; Julio intimidated Carmen through his physical abuse; Carmen tried to intimidate Felix by making her false homosexual and sexual abuse allegations against him; Julio tried to intimidate me through his threatening late-night telephone call.

While intimidation can be an effective short-term strategy in custody disputes and, for that matter, in human relations in general, the fact is that it almost always brings the intimidator down, as it did Carmen. Instead of allowing herself to be frightened into submission, Melody ultimately stood up to her mother, first by telling Felix about the cocaine she discovered and then by revealing all the details of her mother's failures to the court. Eventually, Melody's courage and devotion to the truth prevailed and freed her from the clutches of her lying, intimidating, and neglectful mother. Carmen, for the most part, lost the love and devotion of her daughter and the possibility of unfettered, real-life access to her.

CHAPTER 7

The Delucas

"Three points to remember if you're considering legal action: (1) The legal system has more in common with The National Lottery than a system of justice; (2) The legal system has more in common with The National Theatre than a system of justice; (3) In some countries, the legal system has more in common with The National Guard than a system of justice."

—Tim Field

Nobody who knew Annie and Ralph Deluca was the least bit shocked when it was announced that the two would be separating. Annie and Ralph had been married for four years and, from what friends and family could observe, the four years of the Civil War had been more peaceful. According to Annie, Ralph was a verbally abusive, drunken cheapskate. According to Ralph, Annie was, plain and simple, "a fucking nag." With the exception of their two beautiful children, there was absolutely nothing keeping these two people together and so on January 11, 1986, Annie filed for divorce and Ralph was more than happy to say goodbye.

But not to the children. Because Ralph was indeed an alcoholic and had reportedly once even whacked his young daughter in the midst of a drunken rage, Annie was granted sole custody of Claire and Don, aged three and one, respectively, while Ralph was granted only restricted and supervised visitation. This enraged Ralph to no end and he blamed the court's decision on his ex-wife and thus, over the next eight years, waged a private war against her, using the legal system as his chief weapon. This was a war that consisted of many long and painful battles, including several returns to Family Court (where Ralph accused Annie of all kinds of terrible things) and no less than four abuse-neglect investigations made by the Administration for Children's Services, all of them initiated by Ralph and all determined to be completely unfounded. Strangely, despite Ralph's stated desire to spend more time with his children, his allowed visitations remained irregular and there was even a two-year period during which Ralph seemed to have fallen off the face of the earth, with no one knowing where he had gone and consisting of no contact between him and his children. Still, when Ralph returned, he continued to fight viciously and self-righteously for increased visitation.

Finally, on June 18, 1996, upon his fifth return to the Family Court, Ralph achieved something of a victory. Judge Ellen Richmond, a middle-aged, conservative judge, decided to award Ralph limited, *unsupervised* visitation. Also, according to Judge Richmond, the children would remain in therapy with the psychiatrist they had been seeing for the past year—but now, the parents would be required to participate in the sessions, as well. The therapist was now given extremely wide latitude in improving the children's relationship to their father and the parents' communication with each other. According to the rather unorthodox wording of the Order, the court-appointed therapist now had full authority to treat the Delucas as "he sees fit."

It was a hot summer day and twelve-year-old Claire Deluca was sitting alongside her mother and brother in Dr. Roger Calhoun's waiting room, as her father chatted with the doctor inside the office. Suddenly, the door swung open and Dr. Calhoun leaned out.

"All right now, Claire, Don, come on in!" he called and the two of them rose.

As Claire passed through the doorway and into the office, she felt that familiar twinge of nervousness. She turned to her brother, who was two years younger than she. Don was expressionless, but she knew that he hated the sessions as much as she did.

"Have a seat, kiddies!" Dr. Calhoun said, as he sank into his own large green chair. The children sat down on the couch as their father, sitting in the corner of the room, smiled at them. Dad was always smiling in the office, especially when the topic of conversation was Mom. This struck Claire as odd, considering how much she knew her parents hated each other. There was a boy at school who Claire hated, Michael Winston, and she never smiled when anyone talked about him.

Dr. Calhoun leaned back in his chair and, stroking his mustache with his index finger, heaved a long, exaggerated sigh. "Well, well, well," he said, turning to Claire. "Your Dad tells me you haven't exactly been enjoying these sessions."

Claire stared at her father, accusingly. He just shrugged his shoulders and laughed.

Dr. Calhoun continued: "Tell me, Claire, how happy do you think you'd be if your Mommy had to go to *jail*?" He smiled broadly and went on, "Because that's probably what would happen if these sessions had to stop because I thought she was influencing you too much. I know she must say some pretty awful things about your Daddy, but we're not going to let that get in the way of our progress, are we?"

Claire looked away as the image of her mother, sitting in a cell wearing a striped cap and uniform flashed through her mind. She turned to Don, who was sitting very still, eyes wide, absolutely terrified.

Dr. Calhoun turned to her father and said, "Now, Ralph, what was it you were saying just a few moments ago?"

Ralph leaned forward in his seat, eager, and responded, "Oh, yeah, right, the contract. The kids know all about it. The woman's put out a fucking contract on my life!"

Claire couldn't believe what she had just heard. "What?!" she cried, incredulously. Had her father just suggested that her mother was trying to have him killed? Had he lost his mind? And did Dr. Calhoun have the nerve to put his fingers to his lips and silence her for trying to defend her mother from such an outrageous lie as that? Claire stewed furiously in her seat.

The conversation turned to other matters, with Claire getting more and more angry and upset as it went on. Finally, Dr. Calhoun raised the subject of child discipline. He wanted to know exactly how Ralph was disciplining the children during his overnight visits and Ralph proceeded to describe what he did, but he was unclear and confusing and finally, Dr. Calhoun asked him for an in-office demonstration. Claire couldn't believe her eyes as her father stood up and walked over to Don and asked him to lean over. Then, as Dr. Calhoun looked on, approvingly, Ralph extended his right hand and slapped a terrified Don hard on his behind.

As her younger brother struggled to hold back tears, Claire suddenly stood up. That was it, that was all she could take. This was absolutely absurd and she wasn't going to sit in here for another minute, nor was she ever going to come back once she'd gone. But as she moved toward the door, Dr. Calhoun suddenly grabbed her. She struggled against him, screaming and cursing, but he managed to keep her restrained in a tight bear hug.

Just then, the door of the office swung open to reveal Annie, staring at the three of them in shock. "What the hell is going on?!" she exclaimed.

Dr. Calhoun, still holding onto Claire, responded in a calm, professional-sounding voice: "I'm sorry, Ms. Deluca, it's only eleven-thirty. You aren't due in here until twelve."

And with those words, he reached out and pulled the door shut.

Nancy Schwartz has a reputation for being one of the toughest attorneys in all of New York City. In the mid-eighties, people used to call her the Terminator, but then, when *Terminator Two* came out and the character had significantly mellowed, they took to calling her Land Shark, a reference to an old *Saturday Night Live* sketch. Schwartz may not have been an actual robot or shark, but she was certainly nothing less than a predator in the courtroom. In addition to being famous for her extreme aggressiveness, however, Schwartz was also known for an almost self-destructive tendency to choose the hardest and toughest cases in the Family Court system.

Thus, when I received a call from her one August afternoon, I naturally assumed that I was probably the fourth or fifth psychologist she had contacted, the rest having turned her down. She described the case to me. Apparently, some woman was trying to escape a court order that required her and her children to attend therapy sessions that they experienced as abusive. As she went into more detail, I found myself somewhat moved by the story and, without thinking much about it, agreed to be of service. Actually, it sounded like Nancy Schwartz had taken on a surprisingly simple case. She had not.

When I met Annie Deluca, days later, she struck me as a real salt of the earth type, a woman with a heart of gold. Annie expressed her concern about their court-appointed therapist, and, after speaking for several hours with her children, Claire and Don, I found myself appalled by what I was hearing. Both children described Dr. Calhoun as psychologically menacing, controlling, authoritarian, and even, at times, physically threatening. They resented his coercive and confrontational approach in dealing with them and their mother and wanted absolutely nothing more to do with him *or* their father (according to Claire, Dr. Calhoun and Ralph often ganged up together, usually when one or the other was in the process of criticizing Annie).

Clearly, these children were being made miserable by their therapist, but in order to have a full, objective view of the situation, I found it necessary to examine the written record, which included all of the letters the therapist had written to the judge and other related parties over the past two years. In these letters, Dr. Calhoun described his method as being "a well-known form of treatment called 'confrontational therapy.'" At the time, I had never heard of such a therapy, nor was it listed in any of the three psychiatric textbooks

I consulted (though I have since found passing references to this marginal practice on the Internet).

Dr. Calhoun also demonstrated, in the letters, a clear dislike of Annie, calling her, in his most recent progress report, a "mommy monster" who had brainwashed the children against their father and had tried to undermine the effectiveness of their therapy with him. However, Calhoun offered strikingly little basis for these accusations. In fact, most of his report seemed to be little more than a series of feeble allegations couched in psychological jargon. His claims were rarely supported by solid evidence or reasoned argument and most of what he alleged was based merely on his presumed authority as the therapist–expert who somehow possessed a "God's eye" view of the truth. Additionally, and most disturbingly, the report was lacking any evidence that the Deluca's family situation had improved one iota from the time the therapy had begun and that Dr. Calhoun was making any kind of positive contribution to it.

In short, I found the report extremely troubling and, upon finishing it, immediately drafted a letter to the judge conveying my concerns and advocating for an immediate change of therapist. I was aware that I had been made privy to only one side of the story. But, as I pointed out in my letter, even if the children's description of the psychiatrist was a complete exaggeration, it didn't matter. If after two years of therapy, the children felt the way they did, then the treatment had failed. In one of his early letters to the judge, Dr. Calhoun had expressed his desire to achieve "the unimpeded development of a lasting and meaningful, not just cosmetic, relationship between the children and their father." This goal had clearly and definitively *not* been met.

Judge Ellen Richmond peered out into the courtroom and declared, in a rough, gravelly voice, "The decisions of this court will not be determined by the opinion of a hired gun." That was a dramatic way of saying that the last person who would have any influence on this case would be *me*. In the judge's opinion, I had been brought in for the sole purpose of doing Ms. Deluca's bidding and was essentially an enemy of the courtroom, an enemy of justice, itself.

Having gotten that out of the way, Judge Richmond went on to directly accuse Annie of trying to brainwash the kids against their father and of deliberately undermining the treatment. Finally, she told Annie that Dr. Calhoun, who had twenty-five years of experience in the court system, would most certainly not be removed from the case. As her attorney tried to keep her calm, Annie informed the judge that she would not, under any circumstances, force her children to return to Calhoun. Judge Richmond then put her in contempt and, ignoring Nancy Schwartz's strenuous objections, sentenced Annie to a full thirty days in jail.

The first story to run regarding the Annie Deluca case was a short human-interest piece in a daily newspaper, with the headline: "Mom Goes to Jail for Protecting Her Kids." Soon, there were recurring pieces on the local television and radio stations. In the few days Annie Deluca had been given to get ready for jail, she and her attorney had contacted numerous public officials, all of whom had told her there was nothing they could do, that the judge had not been acting outside her legal authority.

So Annie had done the only thing she could do: she had gone to the press and the story had spread like wildfire. I was interviewed on television about the case, as was Nancy Schwartz. Not surprisingly, Judge Richmond, Dr. Calhoun, and Ralph Deluca all refused to speak.

When Annie emerged from jail, after thirty days, she had become something of a local celebrity. Meanwhile, under intense political pressure, Judge Richmond changed the therapist and was unofficially reprimanded by the Republican Party boss. The Judge had been hoping for a promotion to a higher court. She didn't get it, and was in fact informed that she would *never* be promoted, despite the fact that she had not violated any laws. Her actions, in the opinions of her superiors, were simply outrageous. To put a single mother in jail simply because she did not wish to force her children into seeing an abusive therapist—and a mother who had been perfectly willing to *change therapists* at that—was obviously an inexcusable abuse of power. Dr. Calhoun, for his part, retired from all court work and the law guardian, who had repeatedly pressed the judge to side with the father, was unofficially censured by the Administrative Judge. Remarkably, the Deluca case remained with Judge Richmond, who could now hardly look Annie in the eye.

Annie, following my advice, sent Claire and Don to separate therapists, a situation that worked out very well for both children. The last time I spoke with her, Annie informed me that Claire had not seen her father in a very long time, having rejected contact with him for his previous offensive behavior, but that Don was going on occasional overnight visits with him, which Annie had no objection to. In general, Annie and the children had grown even closer to one another as a result of the whole ordeal. Claire and Don felt extremely proud that their mother had fought so hard for them and that they had all stood together strong.

As for Annie, she was enjoying her newfound freedom, no longer being forced into court every few months by her ex-husband and she told me she now felt vindicated after years of abuse by the legal system. She also suggested I write a book about her case, in the hope that it might help other people in similar situations. She praised me for writing my letter to the judge, reminding me that by attacking the system, we had gone up against great odds. We had set ourselves out on a collision course with the judge, the law guardian, and the psychiatrist, and had ultimately prevailed.

It was nice to talk to Annie Deluca, to see that everything had worked out well for her. I told her I was very happy to see that her family was finally beginning to pick up the pieces and that it seemed that, overall, her case had ended happily. I did not wish to trouble her, so I did not tell her anything more than that. I did not tell her that while the case had ultimately ended smoothly for her, I had had a bit more difficulty and that the judge's final decision, allowing her to change therapists, had been the end of all the trouble for her, but had been just the beginning for me.

For, in early January, several months after my involvement in the Deluca case, I received a letter from the State Psychology Licensing authorities informing me that a complaint had been filed against me by Dr. Roger Calhoun. According to Calhoun, the letter I had written to Judge Richmond criticizing Calhoun's treatment had lacked any valid basis, had assailed his professional competence and ethical behavior, had revealed my own lack of professional competence and ethical behavior, and had demonstrated a lack of honesty.

Specifically, he asserted that I had not reviewed all of the documentation pertinent to the case and that if I had, I would not have reached the conclusions I did. He also lambasted me for not making any effort to verify the credibility, accuracy, and comprehensiveness of the information made available to me. In his view, I should have spoken to him and further investigated the matter by contacting the various social service agencies and personnel that had been involved in the case over the years. Finally, he complained that it was improper for me to have written to the judge without having warned him in advance.

Days later, an investigator turned up at my door to hear my side of the story and I was made to write a lengthy, detailed response to Calhoun's allegations. I would like to say that I nobly and proudly embraced the role of professional martyr for the Deluca family, but this was not the case. Instead, my thoughts at the time were more with my own family and the question of how I'd be able to provide for them if I could no longer practice psychology. Somewhat guiltily, I reflected on the old adage that "no good deed goes unpunished" and then set about composing my letter of defense.

In the letter, I noted that my actions had been governed by three principles. First, I was *legally obligated* to report an abuse allegation and what Ms. Deluca and the children had told me clearly constituted such a possibility (though I had never fully determined or stated that real abuse had actually occurred). Second, I was obligated to respect Ms. Deluca and the children's confidentiality. They had requested me not to contact Dr. Calhoun or anyone else involved with the case for fear of reprisals and I felt I had no right to violate these wishes.

Furthermore, I knew from experience that as a noncourt-ordered evaluator and someone who had been hired personally by Ms. Deluca, it would be highly unlikely that any personnel from any social service agency would give me access to their records or speak openly with me, given the overall context and nature of my inquiries. I also thought it unlikely that there would be anything to gain from speaking with Dr. Calhoun. There would probably be little he could tell me that I did not already know from his written report and he would most likely deny all of Ms. Deluca's accusations, as he had done in the written report.

At any rate, I did not see any great necessity in determining the accuracy of Annie and the children's account of the events because all that really mattered was whether or not the treatment had been a failure, not whether or not anyone had been abused. If the stories were true, then abuse had indeed occurred. If they were not true, still, the treatment had clearly broken down.

Third and most importantly, I felt an ethical imperative to advocate for Don and Claire. Ms. Deluca and her children were in an extremely bizarre situation in which they were pitted against authorities that were insisting that she, the mother, do something that she and her children felt was injurious to them. This was abnormal, unlike anything I had ever come across in my years of professional experience, and I therefore felt a plain and simple moral obligation to do whatever I could to help convince the judge to hear Ms. Deluca out and assign a different therapist.

Months went by as I waited to hear back from the licensing authorities on whether I would be charged with professional misconduct, which could have resulted in the possible suspension of my license to practice. Finally, I received a letter from Albany indicating that I had not actually committed professional misconduct, but had come *very close* to doing so. No further details were given, but I was warned that further activity of a similar nature could result in real professional misconduct proceedings.

I felt tremendously relieved. After going through this kind of investigation, I had a much clearer understanding of why so many professionals are inclined to avoid any kind of advocacy for their patients. As Annie Deluca and I both learned the hard way, it is a litigious culture we live in and if you aren't careful, you're liable to get burned.

REFLECTIONS

Though our legal system clearly has serious limitations in dealing humanely and justly with custody, visitation, and relocation disputes, it usually gets things more or less right in the end—though often at a very dear price to the litigants and their children. One of the most troubling problems generated by the system, itself, is that the families involved are often terribly brutalized by the process of litigation, particularly its incredibly slow pace and inordinate costs, which result in escalating tension and aggression between parents, who feel utterly helpless.

In this bizarre case, we see the system at its worst; a misguided and mean-spirited judge in a power struggle with a plaintiff mother, grossly abusing her authority at the mother's financial and psychological expense; a law guardian blindly going along with the judge and psychiatrist; an egotistical lawyer who wants to win his case for the defendant father, regardless of the ramifications for the rest of the family; a court-appointed psychiatrist taking advantage of his absolute authority to harm the mother and children, instead of helping the children to reconcile with their father. Though this case eventually had a somewhat happy ending, what this courageous mother had to go through in this struggle makes it truly a cautionary tale.

What this case demonstrates, among other things, is the genuine violence that the system can perpetrate on those who use it to resolve their conflicts. While the above story is an admittedly unusual one, it highlights the fact that, inherent in any divorce or custody conflict lies the possibility of everything going wrong—*really* wrong. In a sense, this should not be surprising when we consider that judges, lawyers, law guardians, and forensic evaluators are all ordinary people, with the same limitations, foibles, questionable motivations, and bad judgments that the rest of us possess. Given how many people are involved, the complex matters being dealt with, the high personal and familial stakes, and the extreme emotions that are often generated in everyone, it is nothing short of a miracle that more stories like this one do not occur.

CHAPTER 8

The Sawickis

"Every man must decide whether he will walk in the light of creative altruism or in the darkness of destructive selfishness."

—Martin Luther King, Jr.

The half-rusted shovel cut through the cold, hard, dirt. Eddie grunted, dug in a bit deeper, then moved back and hurled the dirt over his shoulder. He looked down at his watch and sighed. Half an hour to go until Carl would be showing up to replace him for the late shift. Half an hour too long, if you asked Eddie.

At the age of forty-five, Eddie had made it to the graveyard. He'd always known he'd wind up there someday—everybody does—but he never thought it would be so soon. He didn't really mind, though. Digging graves had its perks. For the most part, he didn't have to deal with people (not living people, at least) and, also, working out in the dark had a strange quality to it, almost mystical. It was easy to ponder things, reflect on the meaning of life and stuff like that. Eddie wasn't exactly a spiritual man, but he sometimes liked to imagine that he could hear ghosts whispering in the rustling of the leaves. That was the thing he liked about digging, he figured. You were always alone, but you were never really *alone*.

On nights like this, though, the job just plain old sucked. With the rain coming down on his head, all Eddie could think about was when Carl was gonna' show up. His new coveralls were soaked to the core and there was a nasty chill running up his spine that made him think he might not be feeling too well in the morning. By the time Carl did show up, Eddie was starting to shiver a little. He handed Carl the shovel with barely a word and headed home.

Walking through the front door of the house, Eddie was treated to an all-out assault on his senses. Frank was blowing into his kazoo, creating a horrendous noise. Jack and Suzie were watching TV in the den at full volume. Gail was on the phone, screaming at her boyfriend over this or that. All in all, it was enough to make Eddie want to go back to the cemetery and crawl into one of his freshly dug ditches. But Nancy, who had greeted him at the door, told him supper was already waiting for him. She somehow managed to get the kids to shut up for a few minutes and showed him into the dining room, where a hot meal of spaghetti and meatballs was all laid out.

The children had already eaten, as usual. It was just Eddie and Nancy, and as Eddie wolfed down the meal, Nancy kept asking him questions about his day. This was what she usually did when they ate and it bothered Eddie for several reasons. For one thing, she didn't seem to understand that it was very difficult to chew and talk at the same time. You simply can't answer someone's questions if you've got spaghetti hanging out of your mouth. For another, there was just something so damn *phony* about the whole thing. Because, at the end of the day, Eddie knew, and so did she, that she just couldn't give a shit about how his day was and that she was just asking because, well, *that's what you do*. If she wanted to show him some appreciation for working so hard, the better thing would be to let him eat in peace. He had tried to convey this to her in the past, but it never seemed to get through and he always wound up feeling guilty about it later on.

After dinner, Eddie settled into the easy chair in the living room. Torn apart as it was, this big green chair was really the only thing in the house that Eddie felt like he owned. Everything else, from the bed to the bathroom to the TV, he shared with others, but this chair, this was all his. He leaned back, took a deep breath and started to unfold the sports pages. Most of the kids had gone to sleep already and he could finally have a few moments to himself, a few minutes of peace and quiet.

He was only about a paragraph into Brian Lewis' description of the Knicks-Bulls game, when he was interrupted by a loud shriek coming from Gail's room.

"What the hell?," Gail screamed. "*What the hell,* Joey? You told me you wanted to go—I cancelled *all* of my plans. You can't do that!"

She was on the phone with her boyfriend again, that Italian kid from her class. Eddie sighed. He didn't have the energy to deal with it, so he waited for a second and then continued reading.

But, of course, it was only two minutes later that Gail started up again. This time, she wasn't screaming. This time she was laughing:

"Yeah, uh huh, *uh huh*—good one! Hope you can take 'em as well as you dish 'em!"

"Gail!" Eddie cried out, putting every ounce of energy from his body into his voice, which was still considerably weak. He was exhausted and calling out his daughter's name now felt like even more work than the two graves he had dug that night.

"What, Dad?" came the response.

"Can you *please* pipe down? I'm reading the paper!"

"So-rry!" she replied in an irritating singsong voice.

Eddie went back to reading. About two minutes of silence passed. Then, another two minutes passed. Eddie was starting to get into the article, imagining what it must have been like to be at the game and seen Michael Jordan, the greatest player in basketball history, prove that even after retiring twice, he could still come back and show them all that. . . .

And then, once again, yet another outburst: "Joey, you are an asshole! A *total* asshole! You think everyone wants you—no one wants you—not even me anymore!"

With that, Eddie rose from his seat. This time, he didn't need to summon up any energy. It came to him all at once, seemed to come by itself. Eddie dropped the newspaper onto the chair and started down the hall, toward Gail's room.

Eddie could hear Gail chastising her boyfriend through the door. Calling him lewd names, talking with the kind of language that makes you sick to hear coming from a fifteen-year-old girl. Eddie knocked.

"I'm on the phone, Dad," came the reply.

Eddie reached for the doorknob, turned it. It was locked. No matter. He turned it harder, pulled with everything he had and—*crack!*—-the door came open, the flimsy lock broken. Eddie stormed in. Gail stared at him in shock and he reached out and grabbed the phone receiver from her hand and threw it to the floor. They could both hear Joey's *electronicized* voice calling up from the floor: "Gail? Gail, what's going on?"

Eddie stepped forward, lifted up his foot and stomped down on the receiver, destroying it with a loud crunch.

"Did I tell you to be quiet?" he demanded. Gail just stared at him in stunned silence. "Did I *tell* you to be quiet?" he repeated, significantly louder. And then . . .

"And then what?"

"And then, uh . . . I, uh . . . "

"And then what?" I repeated.

Eddie Sawicki shifted in his seat. His eyes were now lowered to the tacky Oriental rug that a colleague had bought for me as a gift and that I was afraid to replace. Eddie stared at the designs on the rug. He had now gone into a mode I was getting used to from him: *ignorance* mode.

"I don't remember," he answered. "Whole night's kinda' a blur after that."

Sure it was. *Bullshit*, I wanted to say. *You know* exactly *what happened next. You know every last detail of what happened next.*

But it didn't pay to force it out of him right now. The clock on the wall made it perfectly clear to both of us that time was up and I knew there was no way I was going to keep him in the office for even second longer.

Eddie stood up to leave.

"All right, Doc. I'm outta' here."

"Eddie, try and see if you can remember anything more about that night. For next time."

He nodded, wished me a good week and walked out of the office. As I watched him close the door behind him, I thought about what it must have been like for Nancy Sawicki to spend twenty long years with this man, a man who had all the expressiveness and emotional awareness of a brick wall. The answer was easy. It must have been a nightmare.

Nancy Sawicki was born Nancy Williams and grew up in Rockaway Park, Queens. The youngest daughter of a gym teacher and a painter, Nancy had a fairly happy childhood. Her family wasn't wealthy, but her parents were kind to her and her sisters and she had lots of friends at school.

Nancy first met Eddie Sawicki when she was eighteen. She found herself immediately attracted to this tough Pollack from the wrong side of the tracks. Eddie had grown up in Hell's Kitchen. His father, a longshoreman, had been an alcoholic who used to beat him up relentlessly—usually as Eddie's mother looked on and watched. At twenty-five, Eddie had the look and feel of someone who had been through a lot and could handle a lot more. And as far as Eddie was concerned, the time was ripe to settle down, and Nancy was sweet and available, so why the hell not? The two got married on January 17, 1983, and had their first child, Gail, a few years later.

For the first fourteen years of their marriage, Eddie worked as a postal worker, while Nancy did part-time, off-the-books bartending at local neighborhood establishments. But when Eddie took on a second job, working as a gravedigger in the evenings, Nancy quit her bartending. The demands of a large family (at this point, they had two boys and two girls) were simply too much for no parent to be around in the early evenings.

According to both Eddie and Nancy, the marriage had been, from the very beginning, rocky at best. But from the time Eddie took on his second job, the situation began to deteriorate dramatically. For years, Nancy had found Eddie difficult to live with. He was utterly uncommunicative and sometimes even verbally abusive to her and the children. He was also a neglectful provider. Over the years, the electricity and telephone had been cut off many times because of Eddie's failure to pay bills and the family was once even evicted. This puzzled Nancy. With the two jobs he worked, there should have been enough money to cover these basic necessities, yet somehow there wasn't.

But Nancy had submerged most of these questions and complaints for the sake of her family. Her own parents had fought occasionally and gone through hard times, but they never gave up on each other or on the power of the family they had built. Nancy's very conservative upbringing had imbued her with a strong notion that divorce could only be considered as a last resort.

However, by 1999, she had finally had enough. She simply wouldn't take it any longer—she just *couldn't!* Over an early morning cup of coffee, she told Eddie of her feelings. As he tried to brush them off, she told him that she was serious and that she wanted a divorce.

"Are you fucking out of your mind?!" he yelled.

"Eddie, it's not working—I just can't go on like this," she said.

But Eddie would not hear of it. The idea of a getting divorce completely outraged him. After much arguing, the two finally agreed, as a compromise, that they would go to a marriage counselor.

The marital therapy lasted six months, during which Nancy and Eddie accomplished absolutely nothing. Paradoxically, Eddie would admit to many of Nancy's accusations, but, subsequently, he would not apologize or express any kind of willingness to change. By the therapy's end, Nancy still wanted a divorce, perhaps even more than before, but she was now too fearful of how Eddie might respond to the suggestion—especially after having gone through all that therapy (which, in his eyes, had magically cured everything). Big, strong, and prone to long periods of silence, Eddie had always reminded Nancy of a volcano. Even when he would yell, you always got the sense that that was only the surface. That beneath the moodiness and weariness of his exterior, there lay an inner fury waiting to burst out and consume everything around it.

The volcano finally erupted on June 1, 2003. That was the night that Eddie had suggested his daughter Gail speak a bit more quietly on the telephone. After barging into her room, breaking the phone, and screaming at Gail, Eddie smacked her hard in the face and then, in a fit of rage, grabbed a bookshelf from the wall and threw it to the floor, causing it to smash in two. To add a layer of icing onto this spectacular cake, all of the ruckus had caused the other children to wake up and come running into Gail's room, where they got a terrific view of the aftermath. Nancy, who had been reading in the bedroom, also arrived and stood in the doorway next to them. As her eyes darted back and forth between her daughter, crying against the wall, her lip bleeding, and her husband, staring dumbly at the broken shelf as though he were Steve Urkell wondering, *Did I do that*, Nancy made a difficult decision. She hadn't wanted it to come to this, but this incident was unfortunately not the first of its kind, even if it was the worst. This was the last straw and she now knew what had to be done. Several weeks later, Nancy had succeeded in obtaining an Order of Protection and Eddie was out of the house.

At the time the case was referred to me, such was the situation:

Eddie, as a result of the Order of Protection, was legally barred from seeing the children and had thus seen them only sporadically over the past nine months, primarily during several court-ordered visits with a psychologist and on several occasions when he had shown up at the house uninvited. Despite this being an obvious violation of the order, Nancy had not called the police to have him removed on the few times this occurred.

Eddie was now seeking to have unsupervised visitation with the children. Nancy was not against this in principle, but was insisting that Eddie first reconcile his nearly destroyed relationship with them. The children did not want to see him (in fact they wanted very badly *not* to) and so they should not be forced to do so, she said. She reported, as did court documents, that the court-ordered visitations that the children had undergone with their father and a psychologist had been very unsuccessful. Indeed, the write-up done by the psychologist, Dr. Martin Wolfe, indicated that the children had seemed very fearful of their father during the sessions.

They had also seemed very angry, wrote Dr. Wolfe—and according to Nancy, they had good reason to be. In the four months since Eddie had been made to leave the house, he had not paid a cent in child support, forcing the family to go on public assistance and move into a small apartment. This was embarrassing for everyone, but brought particular humiliation to Gail, a typically self-conscious teenager. In addition, when Eddie left, he took the family van with him, leaving Nancy and the children with nothing but a beat-up 1984 Hyundai that wouldn't start.

The children, Nancy explained, could neither understand nor accept that their father, who still claimed to love them, would deliberately allow them to sink into severe economic hardship when he had the resources to prevent this. However, when I spoke with the children, myself, I realized that there was much more to their resentment than issues of money. Rather, there was a long history of emotional abuse and neglect.

"My father's a jerk, plain and simple," said fifteen-year-old Gail, at an early morning session in my home office. "Forget about what he did to me, forget that whole thing—he treated *all* of us like shit."

"Can you elaborate ?" I asked.

"Sure. He would yell at us all the time, for no good reason. He'd completely blow up over stupid little things. He'd yell at my *mom*—and she did *everything* for the bastard!"

"Do you think you could ever see yourself wanting to see him again?" I asked, though I was pretty sure of the answer I'd get.

Gail took a deep breath.

"Let me tell you something," she started. "For fifteen years, he never wanted me around. He didn't give me the *time of day*. So now, all of a sudden, he wants to see us? This is all bullshit. Maybe he's trying to stop the divorce, I dunno', but this is all some kind of game."

Susan, ten, was even more incriminating of her father:

"I don't care if he dies," she declared, her right hand toying with a small green yoyo. "He was a terrible dad—I can't remember a single good day with him. He used to hit me, push me, just 'cause I was laughing or wrestling with my sister or doing something else he didn't like. He treated me like I was a dog."

When I spoke to Frank, aged seven, and Jack, aged five, I had to be more sensitive because of their young ages and opted not to ask them any disturbing questions. However, it was clear from our conversations that they felt no different from their sisters. Frank described his father as a bully and a grouch who wanted nothing but absolute silence and showed no affection.

"I hate my father," Frank said. "He was always either mean and yelling at us or sitting there in silence like an idiot."

Though only five years old, Jack, was able to articulate his position clearly enough. When I asked him if he wanted to see his father again, he said, "No. Not ever."

The general picture I got was of a father who did not allow his children to be children. It seemed to me that he had made unrealistic demands for silence, which hindered their ability to play or joke around and that he had never even made the slightest effort to get close to them and show them that he cared. Instead, he only intimidated them with verbal and physical abuse.

Strangely though, this depiction was not at all in line with the descriptions of the family I had received from their friends and neighbors, who had told me the Sawickis seemed like a perfectly normal and happy family to them.

"They're great parents," said Sam Lewis, a lively and jovial man who lived next door. "Nancy's a great mom, always keeps the kids polite, well groomed. Eddie's no softy, but he's got a good heart and really cares about his kids."

Dave Reynolds, the coach of Frank's basketball team, had similar praise for Eddie and Nancy's parenting skills. He commended Eddie in particular for coming to several of Frank's basketball games and encouraging him and the other children.

These words of praise had me a bit confused and I was left with two possibilities. Either these people had no idea what was really going on or I had been severely duped by Nancy and the kids. Or perhaps the kids had not *intentionally* deceived me, but had been brainwashed by their mother—a sort of thing that happens all too often in divorce cases.

However, for several reasons, I decided that the first option was the more plausible. First of all, I had dealt with lying mothers and brainwashed children before and I did not get even the slightest sense that this was what was happening here. Secondly, Frank, himself, had told me that his father had come to several of his games and had actually highlighted that as one of the few good memories he had of him. "I have two good memories of him," he had said. "He came to some of my basketball games and he gave me a Ninja Turtle for Christmas. He'd be Mr. Nice Guy one minute and then go back to yelling and screaming."

Most importantly, all of the family friends I had spoken to had described Eddie and Nancy as a fairly normal and happily married couple. They seemed to have no *idea* that anything was wrong. Thus, I concluded that looks can be deceiving and that these people were most probably simply ignorant of the truth. Every human being has a private self and then a persona that they present to the public and perhaps the same is true for families. We might invite a couple over for dinner once or twice. We might let their children play in our house with our own children. At the end of the day, there is really only so much we know about other people's lives.

It was at a crucial joint session between Eddie and Nancy that I had my vision. My "vision," as I sometimes call it, is that almost magical moment in a case when the key truths I am seeking suddenly emerge and then, almost spontaneously, everything becomes clear—all of the dynamics, the relationships, the psychological motivations of the conflict—and I know exactly what I'm going to recommend to the judge.

It was a Monday evening and I was meeting together with Eddie and Nancy for what was to be our second-to-last session. Nancy was outlining all of the reasons why the children did not want to see Eddie. In the past, when

I had described her accusations to him, Eddie had always defended himself. He just didn't have the money, he'd say. Not back then, for electricity and phone bills, and not now, for child support. He'd tell me about how every time he did spend money for the family, they'd just want more and more. He'd tell me about how Nancy was using all of the money he gave her for marijuana, though he would quickly back down when I asked for more details on that and I had a pretty good feeling he was making this up. He would tell me that he had tried to be loving and affectionate, but that Nancy and the kids never appreciated it.

Tonight, however in Nancy's presence, he was being strangely quiet. It was almost as though Eddie had never heard any of these accusations before. I wondered if perhaps Nancy had never been quite this upfront with him before, if maybe the relaxed and open setting had somehow emboldened her. Finally, sensing a confrontation might be a healthy thing right about now, I asked Eddie for his side of the story, for his response. He hesitated a moment and then, I detected a sudden change in him. Up until now he'd been looking depressed, deflated. But now, as he attempted to formulate exactly what his side of the story was, there was a sudden flash of something in his eyes—*defiance*, maybe? He turned to Nancy, then to me, and opened his mouth to speak. Eddie proceeded to unleash a flood of emotions I had been utterly unprepared for.

"All right, doc, I'll give you my side, if that's what you want," he said, his voice seething with rage and pain. "I'm up morning and night working two jobs, pushing envelopes, digging fucking *corpses*, and what do I get in return? Get called a cheapskate! A father who doesn't give a shit about his family, who doesn't give 'em anything! You know what it's like to dig a ditch in the winter? In the rain? So what do I get, huh? A wife who calls me a bastard and kids that hate me!"

Taken off guard by Eddie's sudden willingness to express himself, I was without any immediate response. Nancy, however, moved fast with a reply that matched Eddie's exactly in its anger and frustration,

"It's always about you first, Eddie, isn't it?" she said. "Only *your* feelings and sacrifices count, right? What about me? Who got up and made you waffles every morning and had a warm dinner waiting when you came home? Huh? Who took care of the kids, dealt with their teachers, took out the garbage, cleaned all the toilets? I did my share and so did the kids. We *put up* with your moodiness. What about the time you didn't talk to me or the kids for three weeks because when you came home tired, they wouldn't change the channel to Monday Night Football and leave you alone to be a zombie?"

And now Nancy looked down to the floor and I could feel something even more personal coming on. She looked up, this time not at Eddie, but at me. Her eyes were red.

"Dr. Marcus, I would have to *beg* him to make love to me. And then when we did it, it was the most empty experience in the world."

Eddie looked up at the ceiling and sighed.

"What does everyone *want* from me?" he groaned. "I come home from a hard day's work, I want a little peace and quiet. Is that so wrong? How much sexual desire do you have, Doc, after eleven hours of hard labor?"

"Forget the sex!" Nancy exclaimed, looking angrier than I'd ever seen her before. "You talk about all the hard work you did to provide for us, but you didn't pay for anything! I had to get on my hands and knees to get you to pay for the utilities, for the rent. You let us go on *welfare*, Eddie! I know you were mad that I kicked you out of the house, but what about the kids? How could I explain this to them? That we had to go on welfare and move into a shitty apartment because you wouldn't pay the bills, even though you had the money in your pocket?! Dr. Marcus, he's so stingy the judge had to order the support unit to take the money out of his paychecks!"

I turned to Eddie. I was now a bit confused. Eddie was not denying that he had the money—so why didn't he pay? Even if he was mad about being forced out of the home, why had he failed to pay the bills for so many years before that? According to Nancy, Eddie had never spent much money on himself, either, but instead, seemed to just let it sit there. It boggled the mind. A man working two long and hard jobs just so he could hoard the money for no one! Why had he allowed the family—himself included—to repeatedly have their utilities cancelled, to be forcibly evicted, if he had the power to prevent it? It was a paradox, a piece of the puzzle that I was yet to unravel.

"What about all this, Eddie?" I asked. "Is Nancy telling the truth?"

"Yeah, but she exaggerates, Doc. No one understands me. I woulda' given her the money, I woulda' paid for everything, but no one understood what I wanted."

"What did you want?" I asked. "You had a good wife, kids—not a lot of money, but from the financial statements, it seems you made enough."

Eddie didn't respond for a moment. He turned to Nancy, then looked back at me and now his eyes began to water. He started to speak and as he did, the high and mighty wall began to finally give way and at last I got a glimpse of the real Eddie—the weak and vulnerable child that lay beneath the hard, tough, adult exterior.

"You're right, Doc," he said, his voice quaking. "I know she's a great wife and mother. Maybe she'll find it in her heart to take me back. I'm just so fucked up. I came from a home where my father beat the shit out of me for looking at him in the face. Was it too much to expect a little warmth and kindness, someone to make me feel like they cared about me 'cause of me, 'cause of who I was, not 'cause I was some kinda' meal ticket? That's all I ever wanted."

"I gave that to you, Eddie," Nancy replied. "But you never took it in and appreciated it. Remember how I used to stay up late and listen to all your problems? I'd tell you that it would all work out, it would be okay because we had *each other*. The kids used to love you, but you pushed them away, too. You just wanted to take, you never, ever, wanted to give."

"Tell me what I can do, I just need to...."

"It's too late now, Eddie. I've been asking you to change for fifteen years. It's over."

Eddie turned to me, totally helpless. I felt an odd feeling of déjà vu. My sessions with Robert and Jane Gordon, a few years earlier, had climaxed in almost exactly the same way: An emotionally stoic man completely falling apart before his bitter and unforgiving ex-wife.

"She's right, Doc, I don't deserve another chance," Eddie said, turning in my direction, crying outright. "Maybe I can pick up the pieces, Doc? Maybe something I can do could make it right again? I messed up big time."

I nodded. I told Eddie the truth, the way I really felt, which was that he had had it all and lost it and that I wasn't sure he could make it right again. He had decades of pain and anger behind him, behind his emotional and financial withholding, behind his overall inability to give and receive love. Eddie had never given his family anything because he felt like he was *always* giving, even though he wasn't, and he felt like he was never receiving, even though he was. This was the reason he had withheld the money all those years. It wasn't that he couldn't afford to pay for things—it was that it *pained* him to do so. His money, like the green easy chair in his living room, was his, something he didn't have to share with the family, so why the hell should he?

It would take a lot of time and effort to excise all of these psychological demons and I just wasn't sure Eddie Sawicki had it in him. "But if you're going to try," I said, "you've got to transform yourself from Scrooge to Santa Claus. You're going to have to make concrete changes in you behavior—like paying Nancy what you owe her, for instance—and you're going to have to show the kids that you can be generous and giving. It's going to be a struggle."

Now came the hardest part. It was up to me to try to work out some kind of practical strategy for how Eddie would change and move in the direction of reconciliation with his children. First and foremost, Eddie would have to reintroduce himself to their lives in a positive manner. He had been out of contact for a very long time and, while I did not find it to be the case that Nancy deliberately badmouthed him to them, he had inevitably become mythologized as the Big Bad Monster. However, I did not think that any court-ordered visitation (supervised or unsupervised) would be a good idea. The children, at this point, were far too angry for that to work. Moreover, Eddie had neither the self-awareness nor the parenting skills to engage in positive parent-child interactions. But I needed to find some way to keep the channels of communication between Eddie and the kids as open as possible in order to lay the groundwork for a future reconciliation, farther down the road.

My recommendations to the judge were as follows:

1. The children should not be forced to visit with their father at this time. However, mechanisms should be established to facilitate ongoing communication by telephone. The children must not be forced to talk to their father on the phone, but communication of this type should be strongly encouraged. Eddie should also be encouraged to communicate with the children via the postal system, for example, sending cards, letters, small gifts, to which Nancy should respond favorably in front of the children.
2. Visitation (perhaps even unsupervised) could be considered after a four-month period, provided the following conditions have been met:
   a. Eddie must meet all of his financial obligations to the family. Though part of his paycheck is already being taken out for child support, it would be useful for Eddie to provide more than the minimum in order to demonstrate to his family that he is committed to change.
   b. Eddie must enter weekly psychotherapy sessions to help him better understand and alter his patterns of emotional and financial withholding and other psychological issues.
   In the event visitation occurs, the visits should start off as voluntary, with the children seeing their father once a week for daytime visits of up to two hours. Visits should be with no more than two children at a time in order to allow Eddie to give the children the necessary attention and to prevent him from becoming overwhelmed.
3. Eddie must take a course in child development and parenting skills. The course should be approved by the court ideally with my consultation as I knew the best programs. A certificate indicating successful completion of the course should be required.

(As a side note, though I am generally reluctant to mandate psychotherapy, in this case, I felt that it was necessary because without it, it would be impossible for Eddie to alter the behavioral patterns that had wreaked so much havoc. Not only would therapy help Eddie relate better to his family, it would also signal to them that he had realized the error of his ways and was making a genuine effort to change. Additionally, psychotherapy might actually help reduce Eddie's deep-seated pain and anger—feelings which he was largely unaware he even held.)

Judge Michael Cross endorsed my recommendations, and Eddie and Nancy Sawicki entered into an agreement for visitation that closely followed the one I had outlined. Eddie seemed to enter psychotherapy with good intentions, though he had chosen to work with a union therapist who, as far as I could tell, was not fully qualified, but was free. I had indicated in my report that I should choose the therapist, but this point had been overlooked by the Family Court.

I basically lost touch with the family after that. Then, six months later, I noticed something funny. The checks that had been arriving in the mail from Edward R. Sawicki suddenly stopped coming. Eddie and I had agreed that he would pay in monthly allotments and, at this point, he had not even paid half of what he owed. When I tracked him down by telephone, he was perfectly cordial and told me that the psychotherapy was going very well and that he was getting along great with the kids. He then informed me that my bill was *wrong*—and that he had actually paid me most of what he owed, save a few hundred dollars that would be coming soon. It took the intimidation of Judge Cross to get Eddie to finally pay me in full. He threatened Eddie, first with a cancellation of his visitations and then, after that didn't seem to work, with jail time for contempt if he did not pay me everything he owed within the next thirty days. Eddie paid me on the thirtieth day in cash.

After that, I lost touch with the family again, but from what I heard from Judge Cross and the law guardian, the situation did not improve at all. Eddie continued to fight Nancy in court in order to avoid paying child support and maintenance. The visitations went badly, especially against the backdrop of the legal feuding over the money, and the children eventually decided to discontinue the visitations. Eddie's therapist was hardly skilled or motivated enough to be of much use and, in the end, Eddie dropped out of the therapy as well. The last time I spoke with anyone connected to the case, Eddie was considering moving to Florida in order to live near his older brother, Ray. It seems he had finally decided to abandon his "ungrateful" family once and for all and, I imagined, would probably never look back.

REFLECTIONS

Eddie proved unable to use my recommendations for changing himself, which would have been the only way for him to reconnect with his estranged

children. From a psychological perspective, Eddie was a deeply troubled individual on several fronts. First, there was his terrible emptiness and sense
of deprivation, rooted in his abusive and neglectful childhood. Then, there
was his complsive attachment to victimhood (even when he, himself, was really the victimizer), which led to his inability to take sustained responsibility for his mistreatment of his wife and children. Next, there was his obses-
sion with hoarding money, the only thing that could make him feel complete
and secure. Finally, and most destructively of all, there was the boundless
rage he directed at anything that was asked of him, which made it ultimately
impossible for him to attain the one thing he claimed he really wanted—to
feel cared about for who he was. While Eddie did make some transient gestures toward rehabilitation as a person and father, he soon returned to his old
ways and ultimately, being the pained coward and thwarted bully he was, he
bolted.

Eddie's use of money as a form of control is an extremely common phenomenon in high-conflict divorce/custody disputes. In Eddie's case, withholding money (i.e., not paying the rent and utilities, resisting child support
payments, and engaging in endless financial litigation) was a form of emotional violence and blackmail. It was his way of responding to his wife and
kids for not treating him like the "giver" he thought—and only *thought*—he
was. Literally holding the cash in his pocket was Eddie's way of concretely
and symbolically expressing all of this. That Eddie, himself, was prepared to
suffer the loss of basic home services by not paying his bills only speaks to
the severity of his pathological need to be loved and respected. Indeed, in this
sense, Eddie was masochistic, as parents involved in custody disputes often
are. He was willing to suffer for his cause, even though such a strategy further
removed his already estranged wife, and left his children completely desp-
ising him.

Ultimately, Eddie Sawicki depicts the tragic effects of limited self-
awareness and the inability to adequately take responsibility for one's insuffi-
cient and hostile actions towards those one claims to love. Eddie's story shows
what happens when warring husbands and wives are unable to take construc-
tive criticism from their spouses and children and summon up the will and
courage to truly change.

CHAPTER 9

The Masoods

"Fear grows in darkness; if you think there's a bogeyman around, turn on the light."

—Dorothy Thompson

The Karakoram mountains, bordering Pakistan, India, and China, are without a doubt amongst the most remarkable in the world. Home to over sixty peaks, including K2, the second highest on earth, they are often grouped together with the Himalayas, though they are technically a separate range. The Karakoram peaks are sharper, more defined—you might even say more angry. Certain sections, like the Baltoro glacier, with its choppy rows of pointed spikes, or the Lailah peak, which gives off the impression of a giant, snow-capped thorn, seem positively lethal. Then, in stark contrast, there are portions like the rocky valleys through which the famed Indus river runs its course, looking the very picture of peace and tranquility.

Asra and Kamilah insist they can still remember staring out on those peaks and glaciers from the window of a small room in a small house that was surrounded by large trees. Where exactly were they? And, more importantly, how long would they be there for? Nobody would tell them and when they pressed the matter, Bapu would laugh nervously and hush them up, tell them to be quiet around the grownups. Sometimes, he wouldn't respond at all. Did Ama know where they were? Why hadn't she called? Actually, Asra and Kamilah wondered if they would ever see their mother again. It was thoughts like these that continuously occupied their minds as they stared out on the mountains in the distance. Meanwhile, many miles away, their mother was wondering the same about them, growing more and more impatient, more and more fearful, and more and more enraged.

Or was she? By now, it should be becoming clear that in child custody disputes, rarely is anything quite as it seems. The truth is, many of my cases actually remind me a little bit of mountains, themselves. Or mountain views, to be precise. In nearly every case, you have certain aspects that are clear and unambiguous, facts, which are firmly established and indisputable. But then, as you observe a bit longer, you find that beyond the obvious, there are other areas that are somewhat hazier, truths that seem more distant, harder to see with the naked eye. Yes, you know that once you arrive at them, these truths will reveal themselves to be just as clear, solid, and unshakable as the others. But from where you stand right now, they are still cloudy, elusive, threatening at any moment to disappear.

The case of the Masoods represents perhaps one of the most ambiguity-riddled cases I have ever had to deal with in the two decades I've been doing this. In all cases that involve strong emotions and shattered relationships, truth, like its cousin, reason, is often quick to split the scene. But in the case of the Masoods, there were so many areas of uncertainty that it sometimes seemed like the only thing I could count on for sure to be genuine, to be real, was the immense pain these people had suffered at the hands of one another.

Let's start at the beginning or, at any rate, near the beginning. On November 8, 1997, when we met for the first time, my impression of Mrs. Rashida Kirmani was that of a woman who was smart, dignified, and incredibly frustrated. This was our first meeting and I had been assigned the unenviable task of both carrying out her family's custody evaluation and also conducting their therapeutic supervised visitation. Dressed in traditional Pakistani garb, which included a dark green hijab and a long, elegant, cinnamon-colored skirt, Rashida sat in my office on that cool autumn day and proceeded to tell me her story.

Rashida was born in 1970 to a middle-class Pakistani family from the city of Rawalpindi, a twin of sorts to the nation's capital of Islamabad. When she was sixteen, her parents arranged for her to marry Jamil Hassani, the handsome young son of a moderately wealthy carpet dealer. Rashida had mixed feelings about Jamil, whom she regarded as charming, but nonetheless a bit reckless for her taste. Still, her parents had given her little choice in the matter and, anyway, he was a significant improvement over Abdul, the notoriously hot-tempered accountant who had begged her father for her hand a year before.

Soon after the marriage had taken place, the couple moved to the United States, lured there, like so many, by the promise of a better life. After settling down in a small apartment in Brooklyn, Jamil (pushing off his lifelong dream of becoming an actor) opened up a stationery store and Rashida gave birth to beautiful twin girls, Asra and Kamilah. For a while, the couple and their children lived fairly happily, but the honeymoon would be short-lived. Several years after the twins' birth, Jamil began to drink heavily. More disturbing, Rashida would sometimes find little bags of white powder lying around the house. When Jabber, Jamil's second cousin, casually referred to the powder as "coke," Rashida was confused because it didn't look anything like Coca-Cola.

When Rashida eventually confronted her husband about the recent changes in his behavior, about the drinking and the mysterious powder, he was totally evasive. Worse than that, he didn't seem to take her concerns seriously. It was as though getting her off his back was more important to him than alleviating her worry and she found his vague, ambiguous, *half* answers ("I don't know what's in the bag, I'm just having fun!") to be both patronizing and condescending. His whole manner reminded her of the time she had accused him of infidelity, a few years back. Rashida had found a message on their answering machine from a strange British woman who cried and pleaded into the phone for Jamil to "leave your wife, leave the bitch, you told me I was the only one—you swore!" When she confronted Jamil, he claimed the woman was a fellow student in his drama class and that the message was from a scene the two had been rehearsing together. Rashida told him not to quit his day job.

Eventually, when the lying, cheating, drugs, and drinking had became too much, Rashida did what any sensible woman would in her situation. She asked for a divorce. Jamil, probably too drugged out to absorb what was going on, didn't put up much of a fight. Anyway, this would free up his time to finally pursue his acting career. Rashida was granted custody of the kids, and Jamil moved out and disappeared from their lives.

Two years later, Rashida decided the time had finally come for her daughters to meet their maternal grandparents. She had pushed it off long enough and thus, borrowing some money from her boyfriend, Abbas, she and the girls boarded a plane and flew to Islamabad, where Rashida's parents now lived and where they would all be spending several weeks of the summer. At six years old, the twins were becoming more inquisitive by the day and the chance to see another part of the world, their country of *origin*, would be a beautiful thing for them.

The first three days of the trip were like something out of a fairy-tale book. Asra and Kamilah got along wonderfully with their grandparents, who took them to visit some of Islamabad's most exciting attractions, like the Pakistan Museum of Natural History, the Murghzar Mini Zoo, and the sprawling Shakarparian Hills, whose garden terrace offered a sweeping view of Rawalpindi, where their mother had been born.

But on the fourth day of the trip, an unexpected visitor arrived on the scene.

Rashida struggled to overcome her shock as she opened the door of her parents' home to find the man she hadn't seen in two years and hadn't really wanted to see ever again.

"What are you *doing* here?" she exclaimed, refraining from opening the door all the way.

"I've come to see my children—our children. Please let me in."

Jamil had come to Pakistan for the wedding of his first cousin, Ayesha. He had heard from a mutual acquaintance that Rashida was also back in town and he wanted to see his children, whom he hadn't seen in ages. Rashida stepped aside, let him in and watched in discomfort as her ex-husband awkwardly tried to embrace the twins, who barely reciprocated. Oddly enough, though, the girls did seem to recognize him, even though, in his typical apathy, he had not come around to visit them in nearly two years.

"What's going on? What in the world is *he* doing here?" Rashida's mother demanded to know as she stepped into the living room.

"Come, *Ama*," Rashida replied and, glancing at the children once more, she whisked her mother back into the kitchen (Rashida's father was out on a business meeting). Once there, she told her mother not to make a scene, that it was, after all, Jamil's God-given right to be with his daughters.

Several moments later, when Rashida returned to the living room, the awkwardness was still fairly palpable. As the two girls looked on in confusion, Jamil asked Rashida if she thought it would be okay if he took them to the park, located several blocks away. No, Jamil, it would not be okay, she thought, but she could not bring herself to actually say this. As she gazed upon him, standing there before her, unwanted and unloved by his children, she began to feel sorry for him. Anyway, she thought, had he ever been violent with the girls? No. Had he ever abused them or compromised their safety and security? Not exactly, though leaving hard drugs around the house doesn't exactly represent the height of responsibility. Still, he was their father and what harm could come from letting him take them for a short stroll through the park? It might even be good for them to get to know him a little bit. Wasn't this trip all about getting the girls in touch with their roots?

Why did she let him take them? Why hadn't she just looked him in the eye and said, "Jamil, it was good to see you, but you'd best be on your way, you are not welcome here?" These are questions that would come back to haunt

Rashida for a long time after. For after her daughters left for the park in the company of their estranged father, she would not see them again for nearly a month.

What exactly transpired over the next twenty-six days would probably never be known to Rashida for certain. What she does know for a fact is that in that time, she heard nothing from the twins, with the exception of one phone call from Jamil, during which he informed her that Asra and Kamilah were all right.

"Where are they? Where have you taken them?" she demanded

"They're fine, safe and sound," he responded and then put the girls on the phone to say hello.

"Where are you?" Rashida asked, trying to disguise her panic with a voice strained by artificial sweetness. But the girls couldn't really give her an answer and they sounded scared and confused. Rashida thought about going to the police, but she had a grave feeling that if the police embarked on a search for Jamil, he might get wind of it and take the girls back to America, where the three of them might disappear somewhere and never be heard from again. Anyway, why should the police care about locating the girls? They were with their father, weren't they? Did it really matter if technically, according to an American court, Rashida was their legal guardian? No, the best thing to do was to wait, just wait, and hope, and pray for the best, hope and pray that Jamil had not lost his mind completely and would eventually return the girls.

And return them he did, telling Rashida that he had taken them to visit his parents, now living in Shimshal, a remote village in the famous Karakoram mountains. What was the big deal, he wondered. Meanwhile, the girls were totally, utterly traumatized, silent, and withdrawn for days, and Rashida had a feeling that the effects of this ordeal would be with them for a long time to come, even forever.

Five years have passed. Rashida is now married to Abbas, a tall, musta-chioed New York City chauffeur who also grew up in Rawalpindi, but did not meet Rashida until after she had already left Jamil. Rashida works as a clerk in a local pharmacy and the couple, along with Asra and Kamilah, live in a modest apartment in Flatbush. Abbas adores the girls and they love him back, seeing in him the only true father they have ever known. Meanwhile, their biological father lives somewhere in Greenwich village, God help him. They haven't seen him in years and he hasn't given a solitary cent to help the family.

So why is he showing up now? Why can't he just leave them alone and tend to his drugs, whores, and doomed acting career? All right, so seven years ago, a judge awarded him visitation—so what? He had never come to see them, not really, hardly ever, certainly not in the last six years. Why the sudden interest? The twins are so fragile, so *scarred*—do they really need this now? Because at the end of the day, when all is said and done, they are more of a family without him than with him.

I listened to Rashida's story attentively, nodding when appropriate, jotting down notes when necessary, but never betraying my true feelings, whatever they were at the given moment. I did not outwardly agree with any of her sentiments, nor did I express any clear disagreement or disapproval. When the session was over, Rashida thanked me wholeheartedly and left the room.

Now it was time to meet these "fragile" and "scarred" girls face to face. Welcoming them in for the first time, I asked Asra, the older twin, why she thought she was here.

"To talk about why I don't want to see my father, so you can speak to the judge and convince him," she responded.

I wrote this down and circled it, unerlined it in red, too.

Over all, I found the girls to be friendly and articulate as they described to me their enormous, overpowering fear of their father. Asra, the more out-going of the two, told me about the time he had paid an unexpected visit to their home in Brooklyn. Kamilah was out with a friend and Rashida was upstairs, folding laundry, when Asra heard a sudden knock at the door. Assuming it was just Abbas returning from work, she opened the door without glancing through the peephole first and was more than a little startled to find Jamil standing there, instead. Asra had not seen him since the time he had kidnapped her in Pakistan and to face him now, at the entrance of her American home, sent shivers up her spine. He was smiling widely, holding what looked like a box of candy or toys—maybe both. She started to panic, wanted to scream, but right then her mother came down the stairs and Jamil fled.

Kamilah, a shyer, quieter girl, talked little about Jamil, the real man of flesh and blood, and instead chose to focus on the terrifying nightmares she had about him. She described to me in vivid detail the recurring dream in which she is lying in bed, comfortable and secure, when suddenly, a gust of wind forces both windows open and her father crawls into her room from an outside tree branch, his eyes glowing a bright red, his arms waving about, trying to snatch her up. She has had dreams like this one ever since the family's fateful trip to Pakistan.

Both girls attempted to describe their kidnapping ordeal, but there wasn't much to tell, as their memories were too foggy. They could remember riding in a car down an extremely wide road, maybe a highway, the biggest highway they'd ever seen, with nothing but snow-capped mountains in every direction. They remembered the elderly couple, their grandparents, they were told, who were cold and aloof, and who fed them stale Turkish delights. Most of all, they remembered the terrible fear that they might have to stay there forever, in that cold, faraway place, that they might not ever see their mother again, their beloved Ama, for as long as they lived.

Just as I had done with their mother, I listened to the girls' stories and descriptions while wearing a mask of total neutrality, never pretending to feel one way or the other, only calmly encouraging them to continue. But after they and Rashida had gone, I sat at my desk and carefully considered everything I'd just heard. And, at the same time, I looked back on the very different conversation I had had with Jamil a week or so earlier. After much thought, I ultimately concluded that in his claim that his daughters had been artfully brainwashed to totally despise him, Jamil was seemingly correct.

From the moment Asra and Kamilah had walked through my door, I could tell something was off. In their expressions, there was an unmistakable look of determination, as though they were on a mission and were confident they would succeed. This was of course entirely confirmed when Asra gave me her line about coming here so that I could "convince the judge" etc. It was obvious to me that with this cartoonishly transparent statement, Asra was repeating exactly what her mother had told her, namely that the entire point of this session was to *win me over* and get me to convince the judge not to let Jamil visit the kids.

Also rather strange was the way both girls kept referring to Jamil as their "biological father," which stuck me as unnatural and suspicious. In the end, I couldn't help but feel that while their hatred and fear of Jamil was probably genuine, the girls' descriptions of him seemed staged and scripted, as though they'd just spent half an hour preparing with their mother in the waiting room. I had dealt with brainwashed children before and I knew what they looked like and I knew what I was looking at now.

Still, though, even if I could tell the children had been influenced, this did not mean that I now knew the whole truth about the whole situation. If Rashida and her husband had brainwashed the girls, this did not make Jamil a saint and it didn't mean that everything Rashida said was false or that everything Jamil said was true. Unfortunately, not surprisingly, there were more than a few areas where Rashida and her daughters' versions of the events differed considerably from Jamil's version.

For instance, Jamil did admit to going through a period in which he drank a bit too much, even dabbled in drugs and occasionally had "fun" with "other women." However, he claimed that those days were long behind him, an assertion friends and acquaintances backed up. He also charged that Rashida had not met her new husband, Abbas, after her marriage had ended (as she had told me) but *before*, and that she had been having an affair with him for several months while she and Jamil were still married. For a while, Jamil had been too out of it to really notice what was going on, but when he finally awoke to the truth, he discovered that many of his close friends already knew and had long been pitying him over it.

In another area of discrepancy, while Rashida claimed Jamil never attempted to visit the girls in the years since the divorce (with the obvious exception of the incident in Pakistan), Jamil claimed he never had the chance! Almost immediately after the divorce, Rashida moved, without telling Jamil where, making his visitation or payment of child support impossible. I thought it was unrealistic that Rashida would have done this, as it didn't seem likely that she would actively sabotage her own receipt of financial assistance. However, when I confronted her about Jamil's charge, she said, "He could have found me if he'd really looked for me."

Not surprisingly, on the issue of kidnapping, there was a major dispute between the two sides. Jamil emphatically denied ever having taken the girls anywhere without their mother's full knowledge and consent. He claimed that when he'd arrived at her parents' house in Islamabad, Rashida had already known he was in Pakistan and that when he asked for permission to take the girls to visit his parents in the mountains, she was hesitant at first, but after a long discussion in the living room, finally acquiesced. What's more, while Rashida claimed that Jamil had kept the girls in the mountains for twenty-six days, Jamil claimed he had only taken them for less than a week!

Attempts to reach family members in Pakistan were unsuccessful and there was no way to know who was really telling the truth, though I got the distinct impression that the story, as it had been expressed to me by Rashida and the girls, had at the very least been blown way out of proportion. Whatever the case was, as Jamil was now fighting for custody and the girls seemed to have a distorted and unhealthy image of him, I decided that the time had come for them to finally confront their father once again, face-to-face. Though it would no doubt be difficult, painful, maybe even traumatic, it was an experience they would have to endure if we could hope for any progress in repairing this terribly shattered relationship.

But there was someone else who I needed to meet first, without whose cooperation and moderate support, any hope for reconciliation would surely be doomed. Abbas Kirmani had difficulty coming out to my office, as his location at any given time was almost entirely dictated by the two New York car services he worked for. Thus, I had agreed to meet with him at a small diner on Manhattan's Lower East Side, where he would be awaiting a call from his dispatcher at New York Liberty Limos. Over a steaming bowl of minestrone, Abbas explained to me that he didn't like the flakey Jamil, who he had met on several occasions, and that the idea of Jamil incorporating his beloved step-daughters into his reckless, indulgent lifestyle made him profoundly uncomfortable. At the same time, though, he also indicated that he didn't want the girls to be forced into the center of a heated court battle, that he understood the importance of their having a positive relationship with their father, and that he would ultimately be willing to cooperate with my efforts at reconciliation. I liked Abbas, who struck me as intelligent, well intentioned, and somewhat more open-minded than his wife. His pledge to cooperate gave me hope that perhaps this case, so fraught with fear and anger, could wind up being less dissapointing than I was expecting.

The children, when faced with the prospect of meeting their father once again, responded with sheer terror. I could see from the way Asra and Kamilah's eyes widened in horror at the mere *suggestion* of seeing him that this would not be an easy process.

"What if both your mother and Abbas are also there?" I asked.

"I don't *want* to see him!" Asra exclaimed.

"What if you don't have to talk to him? What if you just sit with him?"

"No!!" they both cried.

When asked why they were so afraid of Jamil, the girls repeated their stories about nightmares and kidnappings. In fact, they repeated these stories in the exact same words they'd used the first time, furthering my conviction that brainwashing had taken place. I knew from experience that forcing the children to interact with their father could be counterproductive. However, their irrational fear of having any kind of contact with him whatsoever could not be dealt with at all without initiating *some* kind of exposure, however limited. Thus, with cooperation from both parents and Abbas, I arranged for the children to come to my office and sit in the waiting room as their father sat with me in the inner office. I would leave the door to the office open so that they would be able to see Jamil, but they would not have to speak with him and he, in turn, would refrain from speaking to them.

The result of this first visitation was disappointing and heartbreaking to behold. The girls paced nervously in the waiting room, whimpering and refusing to sit down, as Jamil watched them from the inner office in silence, his own eyes brimming with tears, as well. They absolutely refused to even glance in his direction. It was obvious that even moderate progress would be slow in coming. However, I was determined not to give up. I felt that some kind of reconciliation, however unlikely it seemed, might still be possible, provided I had the Kirmanis' continued cooperation.

I found out soon enough that, to my great disappointment, I did not have it, after all. This fact did not come to me at one time, in a single realization, but rather, as a series of of events that suggested a broader pattern. For instance, repeated phone messages on the Kirmani's machine went unanswered. When I did manage to speak to an actual human being, every date I suggested was impossible or inconvenient.

Rashida, in the few times I succeeded in getting in touch with her, was continuously worried that the sessions would distract the girls from their schoolwork. As for Abbas, who had seemed so cooperative in our first meeting, I could now see that I was dealing with a man who saw himself as locked in a battle for his dignity and honor. Abbas informed me over the phone that he saw no reason why the girls should meet with Jamil, who was an "outsider" to their family, a "vagrant." Jamil should go crawl back into his gutter in Greenwich village, he told me. After all, he'd never paid a cent to help support the family, so what did the girls owe him now?

"He may be an outsider, Abbas, he may be a vagrant, but let's stick to the matter at hand. December 12th—does it work for you?"

"I'll have to check the calendar. I think my wife has an appointment."

It seemed to me that they were all employing the same strategy. They would simply wait Jamil out. Rashida knew that Jamil had limited resources and would ultimately give up the fight when the going got rough. Still, I sometimes thought she might have even felt a little badly for him. Though she belittled him every chance she got and decried the havoc he'd wreaked upon her family by kidnapping their daughters, I never truly got the sense that Rashida truly *hated* Jamil. Rather, it seemed to me that for Rashida, Jamil was little more than a shady character from her past who, like a misshapen puzzle piece, simply didn't fit into her future. His presence was inconvenient—he could only serve as a source of confusion for the girls, and the family just didn't have any room for him in their lives.

As for Abbas, it seemed that Jamil caused him total embarrassment as a constant reminder that he was not Asra and Kamilah's real father or Rashida's first husband. Abbas also felt humiliated because many members of the local Pakistani community knew about what was going on and it made it seem like Abbas had no real control over his family. This was not a battle he could afford to lose and, like his wife, Abbas felt that Jamil would only go so far to see his daughters and would eventually lose heart.

On the same note, the girls, too, were determined to keep fighting until Jamil threw in the towel. In one of our sessions, they even indicated to me that they would rather sit in my office for the next ten years and say nothing to their father than be made to go on supervised visitations with him, which were absolute anathema to them. I found their fanatical stubbornness chilling and when I asked them why they felt so strongly about this, they were unable to provide me with any realistic answers that didn't sound like they came straight from Rashida or Abbas. Still, they had "dug in," bracing themselves for the long haul, ready to stand firm for as long as it would take for Jamil to leave them alone.

Finally, though, after the judge stepped in and put a bit of pressure on the Kirmanis, a date was established for the next visitation. This time, I decided, I had to take things to the next level. The children would not remain in the waiting room—they would actually come into the office and be *together* with their father. True, their mother would be joining them, as well, and they would not have to speak to Jamil, but they *would* have to be with him.

Before either Jamil or Rashida entered the room, I spent several moments alone with the twins, preparing them for what would surely be an emotionally trying encounter. I reiterated to them that their father was not asking for custody or even for unsupervised visitation. All he wanted was to be able to see them for one hour a week, just to sit and talk with them and maybe give them the occasional present. The girls stared back at me, expressionless, as though I were speaking a foreign language and they were waiting only for me to finish.

When Jamil and Rashida entered the room, the girls immediately began to tense up, fidgeting nervously and sliding their chairs over to be closer to their mother. The tension rose dramatically and I felt almost as though the room, itself, had suddenly become electric and that the slightest wrong move could fry us all. I took a deep breath and watched the drama unfold before my eyes.

Jamil leaned into his daughters, who were still fidgeting, still squirming, and, in a soothing, gentle voice, began to explain to them that all he wanted was a chance to be a friend again, to get to know them again. His heartfelt plea seemed to fall on deaf ears as the girls looked away, to no one's surprise. I couldn't help but wonder, though, if perhaps part of the reason they were looking away was not simply out of rejection, but also, because they were partially afraid that he might be telling the truth. If Rashida and Abbas had spoken wrongly and dishonestly of Jamil, if he was not in fact the evil demon they had for many years depicted him as being, was this a reality the girls were willing to face?

"I won't ever hurt you," Jamil stressed. "I only want to get know you."

Suddenly, Asra, with her still turned away, moved her eyes to look at him. And in her look, combined with the very obvious fear, there seemed to be the slightest trace of something approaching tenderness. Jamil smiled.

"Asra. My sweet Asra, you're like a stranger to me. I only want to be your dad again."

Asra stared back at him, that stange look still on her face. She looked as if she might actually speak, but if she was going to, she never got the chance.

"*Liar*!!" Rashida screamed in a sudden outburst. "He's a liar! He's a fake—a phony!"

The girls began to fidget even more. They looked as though they wanted to shrink into their seats, terrified, caught in the middle of all this. I felt an immense pity for them and an overwhelming guilt for putting them through this. However, when the session ended, several minutes later, I also felt an unexpected spark of optimism. The look on Asra's face—it had been real. It truly seemed like she was responding to him, if only for a few moments. It was tragic that the opportunity for further progress had been cut short by Rashida's outburst. However, at the same time, this outburtst had perhaps led the girls to see a new side of their mother, one that it was important they get to see. A panicked, irrational side. Asra and Kamila had seen for themselves just how terrified their mother was of them having a relationship with their father and it seemed to me that this could only be a good thing.

The Kirmanis, as I expected, continued to be difficult. In fact, they got even worse. In one phone conversation, Rashida suggested that she didn't want to distract the girls from schoolwork and that maybe it would better to deal with all of these issues when the summer came around (no less than eight months later!). Trying hard not to sound too threatening, I reminded her that Jamil's visitations were court-mandated. That meant that if she continued to obstruct progress, she could—God-forbid—be threatened with jail time.

"I would gladly go to jail for my children," she insisted. She went on to tell me that this whole dispute was beginning to take a tremendous toll on her family, even creating tension in her marriage to Abbas.

"That bastard destroyed my life once, already,"she said, referring to Jamil. "Am I to let him destroy it again?"

In a certain sense, she had actually called my bluff. I knew very well that it would not be in the best interests of the children if their mother were to be sent to jail. On the contrary, it would be a shameful, humiliating experience that would only further alienate them from their father, in addition to whatever other psychological damage it would cause. Also, to be honest, I was not even sure another visitation was a particularly wise idea. Rashida and Abbas' claims that the sessions were overly traumatic for the girls were not without merit and I wondered if repeatedly forcing the children into this kind of situation, this "lion's den" if you will, could ultimately create more harm than good.

Still, I also felt that I had seen positive signs in the last meeting and was not ready to quit just yet. Moreover, I sincerely believed that the girls' fear and hatred of their father was irrational and that it was truly in their best interests, certainly in the long run, to challenge these feelings and ultimately develop a healthy, normal relationship with their father. They did not have to become best friends with him or even like him. But to continue going through life viewing him as some kind of evil monster, to continue having nightmares about him crawling into their windows, ready to kidnap them all over again, could have untold negative consequences down the line.

A day or so after my last phone conversation with Rashida, Myron Hamilton, the judge on the case, asked me to draft a letter outlining some of the various options for dealing with the situation. Still unsure if any future visitations would be taking place, I imagined that they *might* and offered the following alternate possibilities to the judge:

1. The children should continue the process of being exposed to their father in gradual steps. However, as they have until now gone through this experience together, side by side, it might be worth considering splitting them up and having them meet with their father—and myself—separately. This could serve to weaken their joint resolve to reject their father, making it somewhat more likely we could get them to budge.
2. The supervised visitations should be suspended, as they are unlikely to be successful and to force the children to continue might be detrimental to them.
3. The children should be removed from Rashida's home and placed into the custody of Jamil. This option, while seemingly drastic, has been recommended in other cases of extreme parental alienation by Dr. Richard Gardner, a psychiatrist and child custody evaluator and the man who coined the term "parental alienation syndrome." In fact, perhaps if Rashida were told that His Honor was considering this third option, it might finally knock some sense into her and she might begin to work on opening up the kids to the idea of a relationship with Jamil.

In the end, if I had been bluffing when I threatened Rashida with the possibility of jail time, she had also been bluffing when she told me she would gladly go. For several days later, I received a call from her informing me of a date on which another visitation would be possible.

As I did not know if I would ever get another chance, I decided that for this meeting, we would go all the way. The children would sit in the office with Jamil, myself, and no one else. This way, there would be no outside interference to prevent them from hearing what their father had to say.

The girls arrived at one o'clock, accompanied by Abbas (Rashida had found the last meeting too stressful and did not wish to attend this time). As Abbas sat in the waiting room, I once again attempted to prep the girls for their encounter with Jamil. I told them stories about people with phobias, adults who were terrified of dogs or insects until they were made to encounter the creatures up close and discovered they were not so scary, after all. Once again, I reminded them that Jamil only wanted to see them for an hour a week. and that they would be safe and protected at all times. Once again, they responded with blank stares. The confidence and loquaciousness they had shown in our first meeting was long gone. They were no longer putting on a show for me. They realized I had not given substantial credence to their stories about kidnappings and cruelties and I'm sure they resented me for it.

When the clock struck 1:25 P.M., I knew that Jamil had now arrived at the office. I could only imagine the tension building up in the next room, as Jamil and Abbas both sat there together, no doubt silently, staring at each other like two dobermans, each attempting to establish dominance over the other.

When the clock reached 1:30 P.M and I had said all I could say to the girls, I opened the door and asked Jamil to join us. Taking slow, tentative steps, he made his way into the office as Abbas looked on, bitterly. This time, interestingly enough, the girls did not look away, but rather stared at Jamil. Their expressions were hard to read, though I did not see any of the tenderness I had thought I'd seen from Asra the last time. But they didn't seem to be exactly terrified or mortified, either. The girls also looked at their stepfather and I could tell what they were thinking. Was he really just going to sit there like that and leave them to my and Jamil's mercy? Abbas gave me an unmistakably dirty look as I gently closed the door behind Jamil.

Jamil leaned forward in his seat and smiled a soft smile at the girls, who were beginning to feel less brave and were starting to tremble. It was clearly hard for them to be here, to be sitting with their face to face, essentially alone.

"Why? Why are you so afraid of me?" he asked.

They did not respond.

"I don't want to hurt you, I would *never* hurt you," he said. "Do you remember, Kamilah, my love? Do you remember how you used to climb on your Bapu's shoulder and I would sing to you the song about the red butterflies?"

She didn't respond. He turned to Asra.

"Asra, do you remember the little pink doll I bought for you?"

Asra didn't respond, either.

"The short black hair, the white dress—don't you remember?" he asked, leaning in a bit more and pressing his palm to her small, bony knee.

The touch to the knee proved fatal.

Immediately, as skin met skin, Asra shrieked at the top of her lungs. She then sprang to her feet and nearly broke the doorknob of my office in her panicked struggle to escape. She opened the door and ran and Kamilah quickly followed. Jamil turned to me for a moment, totally helpless. Then, he slowly buried his face in his hands.

I sat there for a second and let out a deep sigh. Then I slowly rose to my feet and walked out to the door, leaving Jamil to his despair.

The waiting room was empty. I found the girls outside on the sidewalk, bawling loudly into the arms of their stepfather. I stared for several moments. I could see then what, in my profound naivety, I hadn't seen before—that the case had been hopeless from the start that Abbas was the girls' only father now and that Jamil was in a fight he would never win with the help of ten armies. From a distance, the view had been misty and hazy. But up close, the facts were clear, solid, unshakable, immovable, married to their foundation as a mountain is married to the earth.

Jamil soon gave up. In the end, the combined forces of his wife's scorn, her husband's jealousy, his children's brainwashing, and his own limited financial resources made the battle for visitation a lost cause. I could only agree with him that, at this point, there was very little to be done and that it was hopeless to think that further efforts would be anything but absolutely futile. The case eventually faded into oblivion.

REFLECTIONS

This very sad case highlights a number of important points that relate to many custody disputes. Firstly, it depicts the dangers of *parental alienation*, a phenomenon in which one parent intentionally and/or unintentionally turns the children against the other parent. It seems quite clear that Rashida and Abbas to some degree negatively influenced the twins' feelings toward their father. However, I would argue that one parent badmouthing the other from time to time is usually not enough to bring about real and total alienation. Rather, it is my opinion that in most examples of alienation, it is a confluence of multiple psychological and contextual factors that ultimately brings the children to feel the way they do.

For instance, in the case of *Masood vs. Kirmani*, the tender ages of the girls, their strong willed and rigid personalities, and their loyalty to their new stepfather, all played roles in facilitating their alienation from Jamil. Also, Jamil's relative absence from their lives and the girls' shared belief—justified or not— that he kidnapped them back in Pakistan, contributed in powerful ways.

Another point put into sharp focus by this case is that what constitutes reality, the so-called "fact pattern" of a custody dispute, is often highly ambiguous, subjective, and debatable. For example, depending on one's point of view, Jamil either did or did not kidnap Asra and Kamilah. Also, while I am quite certain that the girls were indeed brainwashed by Rashida, I can't call it a proven fact, which can't be legitimately questioned. Rashida and Abbas would certainly argue that the girls' rejection of their father was simply based upon their own personal experiences with him.

Parents must therefore understand that what they believe to be the reality or the "truth" might be very different from what the other parent believes or what the court believes. In this context, it is extremely important for parents to be able to step outside of their own points of view and to try and understand what the other party is feeling. If they truly cannot see things from the other party's perspective, they should at least try to critically consider the other argument and the question of whether or not it may have legitimacy or be deserving of empathy. Parents who are unable to do this will be likely to make poor decisions before, during, and after the divorce with regard to their children's best interests. The paramount importance of each parent seeing through the other's eyes is also something that judges and evaluators should always be mindful of as they make their recommendations and decisions.

Finally, another point that is very poignantly demonstrated by this case is that regardless of anybody's good intentions, children often have their own ways of interpreting events and when they decide you have wronged them, it can be very difficult to get back into their good graces. Jamil may have tried to reestablish his relationship with his daughters, but in the end, it was too little too late. Perhaps if he had been more responsible in the early years of his marriage and kept away from alcohol and drugs, he might have built a better foundation for his relationship with them. Also, perhaps if he had not let years go by without seeing them after the divorce, it would have been much harder for them to demonize him (yes it may have been difficult to track the children down, but was it really impossible?). And while I never believed Rashida and the girls' versions of the kidnapping stories, it seems very likely that Jamil, at the very least, behaved irresponsibly. In the end, he was punished for these failures with the worst kind of exile imaginable. He was forever banished from the lives of his beloved children.

CHAPTER 10

The Washingtons

"Freedom lies in being bold."

—Robert Frost

As far as anyone can tell, the early years of Kisha Washington's life constituted about as bad a childhood as anyone can imagine. Kisha was born on March 3, 1989, to Bo and Maya Washington of Morissania, New York, a section of the South Bronx that once prompted President Jimmy Carter, upon visiting in 1977, to declare the Bronx the worst neighborhood in the United States. Kisha's parents were both crack addicts who, to make matters worse, despised one another. Thus, Kisha's early years were marked not only by severe physical and emotional neglect, but also by loud arguments and spousal abuse, as well.

Then, however, when Kisha turned three, the system suddenly stepped in to lend a hand. Kisha was removed from her home by the abuse authorities and placed into foster care. To be away from her feuding parents seemed like a miracle at first, but it soon turned out to be anything but. At the age of three, Kisha was not at the level to understand much, but she was old enough to discover that life in foster care was a nightmare in itself. Living in a small house together with nine other children, Kisha was routinely physically and verbally abused by her foster parents—and may or may not have been sexually abused, as well.

But then, two years later, the system stepped in again. This time, though, it was as if all of Kisha's prayers had been answered. Kisha would not be moving in to the home of some stranger who'd look at her as something less than a pet. This time, Kisha would be moving in to the home of her beloved Grandma Susie. Grandma Susie, nearing seventy, hadn't been a major part of her life thus far, but she had always sent Kisha the most colorful cards on her birthday, sometimes even with candy taped to the insides. Things were going to be much better now, Kisha was sure.

Six years later, on a cold autumn day, eleven-year-old Kisha sat on her hands and knees, staring down at the dusty wooden floor of her grand-mother's apartment, feeling perplexed. She could understand perhaps if there had been nothing else to use, no brush of a more appropriate size or type, but this wasn't the case at all. There was a whole drawer full of brushes, containing everything from large bristle brushes to small, red horsehair brushes. So why then was Kisha being made to scrub the entire surface of the kitchen and bathroom floors with only a *toothbrush*?

Perhaps, it was some kind of a test. In recent weeks, Grandma Susie had commented several times that Kisha was less obedient than the others and somewhat duller (despite being two and half years older than the other two children). Could this then be meant as a means for Kisha to prove to everyone else that she was in fact both obedient and capable? Or maybe it was a punishment. But for what? It didn't really matter, she realized—this certainly wouldn't be the first time Kisha was being punished for something she had no recollection of. Still, it seemed a bit much. When Grandma Susie and Aunt Anna had first handed her the toothbrush, they had both been smiling and Kisha had thought for a moment that it might be some kind of joke. But then, when Grandma Susie had seen Kisha's hesitation, her eyes had widened and the smile had vanished as she said, "Get to it, girl!"

Kisha, a musical child from the start, sometimes liked to let a song play in her head when a chore was particularly tedious. She would let the song play and she would clean, dust, chop, or lift to the rhythm of the music. For this particular task, certainly one of the most boring she'd ever faced, Kisha was scrubbing to the rhythm of "Miami," Will Smith's latest single. As the imaginary music became more and more intense, Kisha's scrubbing became that much more vigorous. Then, at the moment when the song's lyrics turn to Spanish, Kisha's hand jutted out, a bit too forcefully, and knocked into the bottom of the smaller of the two coffee tables. Kisha watched with a mix of guilt and horror as a small plastic "crystal" ball flew off the other side of the table and fell to the hard wooden floor with a loud crack. The noise of the crash was followed by Grandma Susie's loud, angry voice, calling out from the other room: "What the hell was *that*?!"

Before Kisha had a chance to answer, Grandma Susie and Aunt Anna were standing at the side of the couch, staring down at the cracked crystal ball.

"My God!" Aunt Anna screamed, her scaly hands grabbing the sides of her face. "My ball! Cousin Abe *gave* me that!" While Aunt Anna was not quite as intimidating as her older sister, she was much louder, almost as if in compensation.

Grandma Susie glared down at Kisha and asked her, "Did you do this, child?" Terrified as she was, Kisha couldn't help but be struck by the stupidity of the question. No, the crystal ball had been afraid of Kisha and had flown off the table *by itself.*

Kisha solemnly nodded "yes" and Grandma Susie bent down, grabbed Kisha's right arm and yanked her to her feet. She turned to Aunt Anna:

"Well, looks like some girl's gonna need some punishing now. What do you say? Time for another trip to the barber?"

Aunt Anna smiled and nodded. The two of them walked Kisha to the bathroom as she tried to fight back tears. She knew what was coming—they had punished her the same way about eight months before. It had taken Kisha a very long time before she began to look like herself again. Now, the whole process would begin anew. She could see her foster siblings, Sally and Joe, standing in the doorway, watching her. She knew they felt her pain and she was grateful for it.

Grandma Susie and Aunt Anna sat Kisha down on a hard metal stool in front of the bathroom mirror. Grandma Susie took out her scissors and razor and Kisha turned to her own reflection, getting ready for the worst. The tears began to flow as Kisha watched herself begin to look more and more like a boy. When it was all over, she looked in fact like a U.S. Marine. Grandma Susie and Aunt Anna hadn't said a word throughout, nor had they smiled. Their faces had remained stern and uncompromising, as though the whole act had been done solely for Kisha's betterment. That was how it often was.

That night, at approximately midnight, Kisha opened up the door of the room she shared with her two foster siblings and slipped out. At this hour, she reasoned her grandmother and great-aunt should be asleep. Still, she had to be extremely careful. The sharp pain still lingered on in her behind from the last time she had been caught out of her room past ten.

Walking on the tippy toes of her slippers, Kisha crept into the kitchen. She quietly picked up the old, rotary telephone and began to dial the number. She put the phone to her ear and listened. It rang about four times and then, just when Kisha was beginning to get nervous, the voice answered. It was a voice whose significance had always been somewhat ambiguous to her. When she was very young, it had usually sounded harsh or cold. Sometimes the voice could send shivers up her spine. But in recent years, it had begun to soften somewhat and sweeten, almost like a new fruit coming into season.

Now, on the few occasions she was given permission to call, she looked forward to hearing it.

"Hello?" the voice asked, now for the second time. Kisha was afraid it might hang up on her and so she answered:

"Daddy? Daddy, it's Kisha. Daddy, I need help."

When I met with Bo Washington in the Fall of 2000, he struck me as a very gentle man, fragile even, but nevertheless determined. "You must help me save my daughter," he said. Bo had recently petitioned the court for a change in custody for his daughter, Kisha. I, in turn, had been ordered to investigate the situation. As we sat there in my office, Bo described to me in gruesome detail his past life as a heroin addict—and how he had eventually kicked the habit and was now working as a conductor for the Long Island Railroad. He readily acknowledged that he had been physically abusive to his ex-wife and that their lives together had been completely out of control (Maya and Bo divorced in 1992). To save money and to keep himself on the right path, Bo was now living with his elderly mother in Tremont, New York. What he wanted now, more than anything, was the chance to do right by his daughter. He knew he'd been a lousy father and that nothing could ever erase that, but that wouldn't stop him from trying to help her now.

Bo described his mother-in-law as a meanspirited woman, a shrewd manipulator who had managed to "milk" the system. She was getting paid by the government to take care of foster children, but instead of taking proper care of them, she was using the money to support her and her sister's needlessly expensive lifestyles.

Bo begged me to help Kisha. He described to me the daily abuse she underwent. He had actually long suspected something was wrong. Often, when he would pick Kisha up for their bimonthly visits, she would seem anxious or sad. However, he hadn't pursued the matter—not because he didn't care, but simply because he couldn't handle it. Even though Bo had gotten "clean," he was still extremely vulnerable and heavily prone to relapse under stress. Thus, he had put all of the questions and suspicions out of his mind—that is, until the night he got Kisha's phone call and realized he had to face the truth.

The abuse Bo described to me was horrible and vivid. But to get a full picture, I knew I would have to speak with Kisha herself.

When I first met Kisha about a week later, she struck me as sweet but also sullen and a bit withdrawn. It was clear that she did not trust me or the court system, which had let her down so drastically before. However, as time went by and our interviews progressed, Kisha began to open up and I began to catch a glimpse of the hell she had been living in her grandmother's home.

Susie Freeman ruled the house with an iron fist, and no imperfection, no matter how trivial, could be tolerated. Susie, with the aid of her sister, Anna, would often employ the use of sticks, cooking utensils, and belt buckles as weapons for inflicting punishment on the children—often when no discernible violation had taken place. Additionally, Susie seemed to mistreat Kisha disproportionately to the other children, often making her do their chores. When Kisha would ask why, she would answer with responses like, "Because you're special, Kisha" or "Because you're our blood."

One day, Kisha was waiting for the subway on 138th street, when a thought occurred to her. It was actually not the first time the idea had entered into her head. The first time had been when she was riding the big ferris wheel at Coney Island, and it had recurred several times since. While at first the thought had frightened her, she had begun to warm up to it, becoming more and more interested in it, and tempted by it.

As Kisha heard the familiar distant rumbling of the Six train, she stepped up to the edge of the platform. She turned to her left and stared down into the tunnel, where she watched the light of the subway car growing brighter, as the car, with its sharp, metallic exterior, got closer and closer. One small step and she could say goodbye to Grandma Susie and Aunt Anna forever. One small step and all her problems would fly into the wind.

But then a voice, coming from inside her, no doubt—but also seeming to come from somewhere else—said, "Don't do it." And, for reasons she couldn't quite explain, she didn't.

"Maybe it was God talking to me," Kisha told me, as she recounted the story in my office. She had told me earlier that day about how she had been taught to believe in God and the power of prayer by her other grandmother (Bo's mother) Grandma Esther. Grandma Esther was a frail woman, well into her eighties, who would sometimes accompany Kisha's father on his visits and take Kisha to church. Grandma Esther had taught Kisha the story of the Exodus and about how the Hebrews had cried out to God, and about how He had eventually heard their prayers. Perhaps, Kisha thought, if she prayed hard enough herself, God would hear her as well.

"Yes, it probably was God talking to you, telling you not to jump," I told Kisha. She smiled a bit shyly and nodded.

"Yeah," she said. "Maybe He don't want me yet."

Kisha made it clear to me that she did not want to visit or have anything to do with Grandma Susie anymore. The only reason she had hesitated to say anything until now was because she was afraid of reprisals. Several years before, Susie and Anna had been investigated on charges of inadequate guardianship and lack of medical care, though neither charge had held up in court. Those few months had been a very tense time for Kisha and the other children, and each child had been threatened with serious repercussions if they told the abuse authorities anything incriminating. Kisha had only agreed to talk now because her father had promised his full support. There had been a time when a promise from her father meant nothing at all, but that, it seemed to her, was in the past.

On the subject of contact with her mother, Kisha was less rigid. She was willing to embark on the occasional visit with her mother, but did not want it to be court ordered. Maya had recently been released from prison, where she'd been sent for attacking a man with a nail file. Kisha was not really afraid of being physically hurt by her mother, but complained that Maya couldn't seem to stay focused on her and would often entertain strange men while Kisha was visiting. However, she did not want to shut her mother out completely and said that she still loved her, and felt sorry for her. She wanted to continue to have some visits with Maya and wanted these visits to be arranged through Bo.

Sensing that Kisha's grandmother would deny all the allegations (the idea of Susie saying, "Why, yes, I abuse Kisha, just like I abuse all my children!" seemed somewhat implausible), I decided I should interview a non-biased third party. Someone who knew both Kisha and her grandmother but was not really personally involved with, or affected by, either of their lives.

I found such a person in Jose Torres, the superintendent of Susie Freeman's building. Jose, a middle-aged man with an easy smile, spoke only Spanish, so I arranged to have a translator present at our meeting. Jose told me that Kisha's grandmother was universally disliked in the neighborhood and that it was well known that she treated Kisha and the other foster children like slaves. He had overheard Kisha and the other children on several occasions complaining, and sometimes crying, about the abuse. He had also frequently heard loud cursing coming from the apartment, though he had no actual evidence of any *physical* abuse. He also said that he had no idea how the grandmother could afford the apartment, since no one seemed to work (aside from taking care of the kids), and he speculated that Susie and Anna were probably cheating welfare.

After a short interview with Ellen White, a seventeen-year-old neighbor, confirmed much of what Torres had said, I decided that I was near the end of my investigation. There was only one crucial interview left: Susie Freeman herself.

When Susie Freeman entered my office, I was struck first and foremost by her diminutive size. At four-foot-nine, Susie looked like the stereotypical "little old lady" that one might help across a busy thoroughfare. However, if I'd learned anything in my years as a custody evaluator, it was that looks are often deceiving. Anyway, it was only minutes into our interview that the ruthless authoritarian underneath the gentle exterior began to emerge.

"Dr. Kenilworth, it's the same thing over and over again!" she exclaimed. Despite her full knowledge that my last name was Marcus, she insisted on calling me Dr. Kenilworth because that had been the name of the doctor who had investigated her regarding the previous abuse allegations. Susie wanted to emphasize that this was just a pointless continuation of that episode and that Dr. Kenilworth and I were interchangeable, and that neither of us would find anything relevant. Susie denied all of Kisha's claims and insisted that it was Kisha's father who was behind all this, a useless drug addict who had always been jealous of her close relationship with his daughter.

When I went through each of Kisha's allegations, Susie had an entirely different version of each story and an explanation why Kisha might want to lie about it. "I find it ridiculous that the court is listening to an eleven year old child who never complained before," she said. She repeatedly emphasized that there was no proof of any wrongdoing, only unsubstantiated "fairy tales." She also showed me a drawing Kisha had made for her, which was supposed to indicate to me that Kisha held positive feelings for her. The drawing was dated 1995, five years ago, but I chose to hold my tongue.

Susie also pointed out that Kisha had been doing fairly well in school, which indicated that she was probably not being abused. I did not buy this line of reasoning at all. Sure, sometimes children let their grades fall because of problems in the home. Other times, however, the problems in the home propel the children to escape into their schoolwork. Again, however, I chose to refrain from argument and react as though I agreed. In general, I thought it would be best for the safety of Kisha and her foster siblings if I pretended that I was going to side with Susie against Kisha's father. However, despite my best efforts, I got a strong sense that Susie was not the least bit fooled. This meant that Kisha and the others could be in jeopardy. And that meant I had to act fast.

Almost immediately after my meeting with Kisha's grandmother, I telephoned the judge "off the record," and shared with him some of my concerns. Afterward, I wrote him an official letter describing my findings in more detail, which I personally delivered to him right away. It was a Friday and so the judge ordered an emergency conference to be held early Monday morning. The court contacted all of the parties and on Monday, Kisha, her father Bo (whom Kisha had been visiting for the weekend), his lawyer, Kisha's paternal grandmother, and myself all arrived at the family court.

Susie Freeman had been contacted but was nowhere to be seen. The Judge held a hearing and then, largely based on Susie and her lawyer's absences (without any explanation or justification) granted physical and legal custody to Kisha's father. He also ordered an emergency investigation into Ms. Freeman's home, for the sake of the other foster children. The foster children were subsequently removed from Susie's care and she and her sister Anna came under investigation by the welfare and foster care authorities, in addition to the Bronx District Attorney.

As far as I know, Grandma Susie and Aunt Anna were removed from Kisha's life forever, something that delighted Kisha. Her mood improved dramatically and she found herself happier than she'd ever been, living with her father and her Grandma Esther. With Grandma Esther's encouragement, Kisha became heavily involved in the local church, doing charity work and recreation, and about a month after the case had been closed, I received the following letter in the mail:

Dear Dr. Marcus,

Thank you for believing in me and I thank God for sending you to help me get out of Egypt land. I am very relieved and happy that I am finally with my father and grandmother. Now that the stress from the court case is over, I am sure that my average will go up next term. The story of Moses taught me the Power of God and to always keep my faith because all things work together for Good to those who love Him. May you and yours always have the never ceasing favor of God. This is our prayer for you.

Sincerely,

Kisha

REFLECTIONS

Kisha's letter, and, for that matter, her entire life struggle to free herself from Grandma Susie and Aunt Anna, is nothing less than a hymn of praise to the glory of God. Her incredible triumph is a testament to her inner strength, faith and resourcefulness, and a demonstration of true courage. Being "raised" by drug-addicted parents, having to endure the abuses of foster care and the ineptitude of child protective agencies, and, of course, having to survive the brutality of her cruel grandmother and great Aunt, Kisha truly went up against heavy odds. Her story reminds us that sometimes, despite everything (including natural vulnerabilities, doubts, and confusions), a child's hidden beauty, will power and noble character will prevail.

Kisha's story also teaches all of us involved in the tragic world of child custody conflicts—parents, teachers, law guardians, forensic evaluators, and judges—about the importance of listening to the child. Indeed, from the beginning to the end, this tale speaks to the necessity of "'paying heed' to another's speech." It was the voice from within that told Kisha not to throw herself in front of the number Six train; it was Kisha's desperate plea to her father that night on the telephone that mobilized him to finally help her (just as it was his comforting voice and reassurance that gave her hope and courage); it was Kisha's pained words to me in my office that got me to believe her; finally, it was a compassionate judge who *listened* to my advice, despite there not being enough "hard evidence" to justify immediately removing Kisha and the other children from Grandma Susie's custody.

It must be noted, however, that in dealing with children in custody conflicts, it is a special quality of attentiveness that is necessary, a form of listening that involves more than simply acquiring knowledge *"about"* the child, but rather, involves learning *"from"* the child. That is to say that we must attempt to be "moved," "touched," and "affected" by the child's words.[1] Only through such genuine empathy with the child, can we adults take the responsible actions and do the right thing.

---

[1] Told, Sharon. *Learning from the Other. Levinas, Psychoanalysis, and Ethical Possibilities in Education.* Albany: State University of New York Press, 2003, pp. 111, 118, 134.

Conclusion

"We are made wise not by the recollection of our past, but by the responsibility for our future."

—George Bernard Shaw

In each of these ten cases, we have tried to convey something of the depth and magnitude of the terrible suffering that individuals often have to endure as a result of broken marriages or failed relationships. A child custody dispute clearly adds an extra layer of pain to this equation and in almost all such conflicts the effects are psychologically hurtful in some way or another. As Judith Wallerstein and other divorce researchers have pointed out, these negative effects are not necessarily transitory. Rather, there is often profound long-term psychological scarring on the divorcing parents and, most assuredly, on their children. Additionally, divorce and custody disputes are frequently financially calamitous affairs, particularly for women, who tend to wind up significantly worse off than men. There is evidence to suggest that roughly one third of all divorces result in the woman involved spending some time below the poverty line.

Though each of the stories presented in this volume is unique in its own way, most have at least one common factor: parents who allow their own selfish needs to override the needs of their children. For example, in Chapter 8, Eddie Sawicki claims he loves his family, but he is nevertheless unwilling to help them out financially or to become more emotionally generous and less consumed by his rage. His anger at his wife for neither being appreciative enough of his sacrifices, nor servile enough to his infantile needs, hurls his marriage and family into disarray. In Chapter 4, Maria Stallone claims to be acting in the interests of her son, but her need for control and her hatred for her ex-husband cause her to kidnap the boy and disappear into a life of anonymity.

Whether the result of an inherent character flaw or a contextually determined response to a painful and complicated situation, these parents' inordinate needs for self-validation—their moral outrage, hurt, and pathological compulsion to "win" at all costs—wreaked havoc on the lives of their loved ones. It should be noted that while it is obvious that such selfish behavior is severely detrimental to the children, it can also have other unintended consequences that ripple through the entire family system, creating additional chaos and pain that were never even anticipated.

What then have we learned from these ten cautionary tales? We will now briefly describe four essential "take home" points, simple words of advice about one's attitude that may assist parents in avoiding, or at least reducing, their and their children's "useless suffering."

(1) *Determine Your Attitude Toward the Other:* Most important in this effort at "damage control" is to decide in advance on an overall attitude toward one's spouse or significant other in the ensuing legal conflict. Will it be reasonable and compromising, keeping at the forefront the best interests of the children? Or will it involve the loss of a sensible perspective, resulting in the sacrifice of the children's well-being and a destructive engagement with one's former partner or spouse? While we are aware that what constitutes "reasonable," "compromising," and "best interests of the child" are all in the eyes of the beholder—and ultimately, the Judge—the parent must be aware of this as well and understand that in most cases, everything comes down to one's perspective. Such a view will automatically put one in a position to think outside of their own hurt and anger and will keep them from falling prey to perception-distorting emotions that can lead to very poor decision-making throughout the custody dispute.

(2) *Determine Your Attitude Toward Yourself:* A related and necessary way to avoid much of the destructive fallout that comes from a contentious custody conflict is to develop and maintain a self-critical attitude. By "self-critical," we refer to the capacity to take an honest and impartial look at oneself, perhaps with the help of a friend or psychotherapist, and to acknowledge—and, where possible, *correct*—one's faults as they relate to one's marriage, children, divorce, and custody dispute. This inner sense of responsibility will make it less likely that one will simplistically blame one's spouse and try to externalize all of the faults onto others.

The right attitudes, combined with patience and self-control, will likely prevent, or at least reduce, the possibility that a parent will do some of the worst things described in these cases. That is, armed with the right attitudes toward the other and toward oneself, a parent will not (a) try to turn their children against the other parent (e.g., parental alienation), or use the children as messengers and spies; (b) badmouth one's spouse in front of, or in earshot, of the children; (c) make false allegations of neglect or abuse against the other parent, for the sole purpose of strengthening their legal case in court; (d) interfere with the other parent's visitation or in any way attempt to obstruct measures meant to improve their relationship with the children.

Indeed, as the cases presented in this book have shown, the list of what *not* to do if one loves one's child, can go on and on. On the flip side, a parent who embraces the right combination of attitudes will (a) sincerely consider what the children want, especially if they are of a mature age (as teenagers are); (b) accept that in many instances, young children should live with the parent who has done most of the actual everyday parenting; (c) accept the fact that custody arrangements need to be periodically reevaluated over time depending on the ages of the children and their needs. In other words, this is not a winner-takes-all game, as the adversarial legal system tends to make parents feel. For example, a fifteen-year-old boy who has always lived with his mother, but decides that it is time to see what it would be like to live with his father, should be allowed to do so (assuming the father is competent) even if the mother feels distressed and abandoned by the change and hates her ex-husband. Sometimes what is right for the child at a particular time in his or her development may not feel just to one or more parent. This is a brutal fact both parents must learn to accept.

(3) We are well aware that even if one embraces the correct attitudes, as described above, one may find oneself faced with a belligerent and mean-spirited spouse, who may even be mentally unsound. It is extremely difficult to be reasonable and compromising with a brute and bully whose main goal is to bring you down, to hell with the children (despite their lip service to the contrary). In such situations, the antagonistic parent may want to attempt to exact reprisals against the other one, perhaps through the children or by pulling the more reasonable parent into a series of skirmishes that could relate to issues such as child support, maintenance, visitation scheduling, etc.

Sometimes in these contexts, the antagonistic parent attempts to reargue and replay the very problems and dynamics that existed when the parties were still living together and which led to the separation—unfinished personal business that by definition cannot be finished until the other parent is dead or destroyed. Often, the antagonistic parent may attempt to use power-ful legal weaponry against the other. In all of these instances, it takes noth-ing short of heroic restraint to maintain focus and perspective and keep the children's best interests first and protecting oneself second. It will probably require the help of a psychotherapist experienced in such matters or a trusted friend to keep a reasonable personal orientation in the face of this adversary who most likely knows one's personal weaknesses quite well. Heroic restraint, not allowing oneself to be internally provoked (what the Taoists call "non-action") is frequently the most effective way to respond in these kinds of situ-ations. Still, sometimes, with the help of an effective "ball-busting" lawyer, a parent must face down spousal violence with even greater violence, an ugly truth of the custody wars.

(4) Finally, as it should by now be apparent (and as many Judges have told warring parents in the court room), the legal system, as it currently stands, is not a very civilized or effective tool for resolving custody, visitation, or re-location conflicts. It is painfully slow, significantly overburdened, ill suited for sensitive handling, and extremely costly. In addition, despite a lot of talk about the "best interests of the children," within the system, children are still, both legally and psychologically, the most unprotected and vulnerable parties in the conflict, though there has been some progress made of late. Perhaps in time, the system will be reformed and we agree with those scholars such as Mary Ann Mason, who have advocated the creation of a new, comprehensive family court system as the best way to fix this problem.[1]

But given the fact that the system is still badly broken and limited in its effectiveness, there are two alternatives to the courtroom that parents ought to consider before they enter into the "twilight zone" of the custody wars. The first is "mediation," a process in which parents, with the help of a pro-fessionally trained mediator, attempt to resolve their issues on a level playing field and come to an agreement that is then memorialized in writing. Outside lawyers should of course look over the final agreement before it is signed.

Second, there is an approach known as "collaborative law." In this ap-proach, each parent finds their own lawyer and the two lawyers then agree to negotiate a solution with an attitude of compromise and cooperation. Such collaborative lawyers work to help resolve issues and do not litigate for you. Thus, the whole ambience of negotiation is gentler and kinder as compared

---

[1]Says Mason, "the greatest advantage of a comprehensive family court would be a better fo-cus on the best interests of the children. The best aspect of the juvenile court—social support services [parent education, child care, and counseling], representation, and long term mon-itoring of families in crisis could be offered to all children and their parents." *The Custody Wars*. New York: Basic Books, 1999, p. 233.

with the traditional adversarial approach.[2] There are many good books out
there that describe mediation and collaborative law in greater detail. In our
view, both of these options are by far more humane, effective, and inexpen-
sive ways of sorting out your custody dispute than the adversarial method. It
is a decision between cooperation and combat and the smart choice is obvious.

Whatever approach one takes to resolving their custody dispute, in the end,
it really comes down to one simple question: What matters more to you? Winning the battle *against* your spouse or winning the battle *for* your child? For,
to paraphrase the late Israeli Prime Minister, Golda Meir, only when parents
learn to love their children more than they hate each other, can the kinds of
tragedies memorialized in this book cease to occur.

---

[2]A court-appointed Parenting Coordinator (PC), a licensed mental health professional, attorney or family mediator with specialized training in parenting coordination can be very
helpful for those parents who have difficulty because of ongoing conflicts between them.
The PC helps "high conflict" parents implement their agreements and court orders, trouble shoots, and acts as an informational resource. It is essential that the PC be a "binding
arbitrator" in those domains under his court-ordered mandate.

About the Authors

JOSEPH HELMREICH is a screenwriter, journalist, and musician. A graduate of Rutgers University, he lives in New York City and works in International Film Distribution for The Weinstein Company.

PAUL MARCUS is a psychologist and psychoanalyst. The author or editor of nine books, he has been a forensic evaluator in child custody cases before New York State's Family and Supreme Courts for more than twenty years. A diplomate in child custody evaluation from The American College of Forensic Examiners, a founding member of the Parenting Coordinators Association of New York, and a supervising and training analyst at the National Psychological Association for Psychoanalysis, he lives with his wife and two children in New York. He has been a faculty member at New York University, Queens College, and at The University of London.